Going Fishing

To Reggie Bruce.

*I have dedicated this book to you.
There is not a fish in it too big to
be believed, or too small to be kept.
As you suffer from "fish-trouble"
yourself, you will appreciate its
originality, in so far that on one
or two occasions—I did not let that
big one get away.*

Negley

"Silverbanks,"
1942.

To

Reggie Bruce.

I have dedicated this
book to you. There is
not a fish in it too big
to be believed, or too small
to be kept. As you suffer
from "fish-trouble" yourself
you will appreciate its originality, in so far that on one
or two occasions — I did
not let that big one get
away.

[signature]

"Sedgebanks"
1942

Where the dark rivers curve down from Exmoor

Going Fishing

Negley Farson

Illustrated
by
C.F. TUNNICLIFFE

Hamlyn Paperbacks

GOING FISHING
ISBN 0 600 20765 X

First published in Great Britain 1942 by Country Life Ltd
This edition first published 1981 by Clive Holloway Books, London
Hamlyn Paperbacks edition 1983

Copyright © 1981 by Daniel Farson
Colour plates Copyright © 1981 by Clive Holloway

This edition produced for Hamlyn Paperbacks by
Clive Holloway Books

Hamlyn Paperbacks are published by
The Hamlyn Publishing Group Ltd,
Astronaut House,
Feltham,
Middlesex, England

Flies tied by Stewart Canham and photographed by Bryce Attwell
Dedication note from Negley Farson to Reginald Bruce
reproduced by kind permission of Jack Heddon

Printed and bound in Hong Kong by Elin Printing Co Ltd

Introduction

I first read *Going Fishing* in 1943 when, as a prisoner-of-war, I was serving a term of solitary confinement following an escape attempt and a friendly guard smuggled the book into my cell. For a couple of months it was my only literature, so I can claim to have read it pretty thoroughly! But Negley Farson proved more than a solace; he was a revelation. Of all the fishing books I had read, his was the best.

It still is.

Hugh Falkus
Cragg Cottage 1981

FOR
REGINALD BRUCE
OF
ELMHURST FARM

Statement

This is just a story of some rods, and the places they take you to. It begins with surf-casting on the New Jersey coast, when I was thirteen, and carries on to such scenes as fly-fishing the headwaters of the Kuban in the upper Caucasus, and casting for rainbow trout in the rivers of southern Chile, with a volcano erupting every ten minutes within plain view. There is not a record, or even a very big, fish in it; and some of the finest things fishing has given me I have found beside the streams of the West Country in England. I do not know the names of a tenth of the flies in the book, and thank the Lord I don't want to. I would not be at all upset if you opened my own fly-boxes and showed me a dozen strangers. I did not know the name of the finest fly I ever had, nor did the man who tied it; he was an English captain in the Army of Occupation, at Cologne, and he said it had worked well for him in southern Germany. After a prodigious career, a trout took it away from me one night in the Balkans. What I do know are a couple of dozen old reliables, and I think I know where and how to use them. As time goes on I shall add others to this coterie, when I've found them useful. I love rods, I suppose, with the same passion that a carpenter, a violinist, or a Monaco pigeon shot love their implements. I love using them. But, if I can't, I can get a lot of fun by just taking them out of their cases and looking at them. A pair of trout rods helped to keep me alive when I was facing a riddle of poverty out in British Columbia where they provided free food; and I've used them for politics-to make a wild Irishman talk, when he wouldn't have otherwise. Although I once thought I was going to come to no good through fishing, I've even made money out of it-my little 'Duplex' rod has provided me with many articles. But chiefly I love rods because of their associations, the places have brought me to. They have been part of my kit, when I travel, for many years. This magic wand has revealed to me some of the loveliest places on earth. That is the story of this book.

Negley Farson

List of full page illustrations

Colour Plates of Maps and Flies

(The Flies are named from left to right as they lie on the map)

Contents.

Going Fishing

I

The early days; surf-casting along the New Jersey sands;
the Cattyrackers of the Delaware Bay; and
the wild geese of the Carolinas

I went into the hazel wood   *And when white moths were on the wing*
Because a fire was in my head.   *And moth-like stars came fluttering out*
I cut and peeled a hazel wand   *I threw the berry in a stream*
And hooked a berry on a thread   *And caught a little silver trout.*

The New Jersey coast lay bleaching under the winter sun. The lighthouse blazed like a white bone. The dune grass stood still. And the green ocean lay like a pond. There were no foot-marks along the sand.

The summer was over, one of those long summers of childhood. I was walking along the tide mark, examining the driftwood and wreckage cast up by a recent pounding storm. There was always mystery in these bits of broken timber and rusted metal, some of which had been lying off the beach for years. The strewn, irregular line of the highest surge of waves was a continuous story after each storm. But I was searching for a specific treasure. It was always the same; a particular type of tackle that we used off that coast—a triangular brass swivel, to one end of which would be left, usually, a broken bit of parted Cuttyhunk line; a three-ply twisted gut leader from another loop; and a four-ounce pyramidal sinker dangling from the other.

This was the rig of the surf-casters, those men who waded far out into the sea, and cast with a stout two-handed greenheart or snakewood, far out, hundreds of feet beyond the on-rushing combers, to where the great striped channel bass lay crunching clams in the dappled lagoons of the sea floor. I found this tackle, entangled around waterlogged planks or twisted in some conglomerate wreckage, chiefly because of the delicacy of this sport. For, making a full-armed cast with the big quadruple reel, this four-ounce sinker was slung like a bullet into the sky. You controlled the spinning reel with your thumb, barely braking; and, if you had a back-lash when the sinker was in full flight—even the Cuttyhunk parted.

You stood there, watching helplessly, as your tackle sailed outwards, having severed all connections with you, to drop into the open sea. Sometimes a channel bass, or a flounder, or a weakfish would take the clam or bit of shedder-crab with which the hook was baited, and ultimately die. These, too, were washed ashore. The storms dug into the sea sands and beat everything up. We once found part of a yard of an old sailing ship. And it was ripping and snarling at one of these bits of decayed fish that I found Joe. The fish was a monstrous thing, with a mouth about a foot wide, ugly teeth, all head, and no tail; we used to call them 'all-mouths.' Joe was the doughtiest bull terrier I have ever encountered.

As I said, the summer was over. Joe was a castaway himself. I'd like to know what sort of a person his master was, for some people did leave their dogs and cats when they went away. And Joe seemed to have been soured by it. He had, for several days, a grudge against all mankind. But I was out of a dog at that moment, and so a flirtation ensued that took me the better part of a dangerous afternoon. The end of it was that Joe followed me home, his hackle rising every time I turned to speak to him, until I got him into the backyard, and shut the gate. Joe was caught.

This was perhaps the finest channel bass season, this tail-end of autumn; and with the setting in of real winter the 'frost fish' would come up along the coast, and there would be night after night when, with a bucket of long-necked clams, I would go out and fish for ling. Joe accompanied me, sitting by my side on moonlit nights, pondering in his dog-way, over the mysteries and melancholy of the lonely sea.

It said so many things to me! It was over thirty-five years later, out on Lake Victoria in Uganda, when I had some natives tell me, wide-eyed, their legends of the Sese Islands (they said to me they had no special name for every kind of fish, they were just 'the Things in the Water') that I touched again the fringe of this imagination which used to thrill, depress, and fill me with such breathless meditation on those enchanted nights. I pictured the sea's depths and filled them with every shape, any of which I might hook; these Things in the Water.

That was the right name for them. In the long native canoe on Lake Victoria, I was still wondering what we would catch. The water still held mystery. The anxiety had not diminished. It has not yet.

In those early days fishing was uphill work. There was a certain amount of ignominy attached to it. It was too often associated with failures, with ne'er-do-wells, with not-getting-on; and, in our Calvinistic civilisation, where to be poor was considered almost a crime, such a waste of time as fishing was considered unpardonable. The result was that some of the finest men I have ever known were fanatic fishermen. It took, for some people, great courage.

The female members of my family would rather eat *anything* from the fishmonger than what I caught. For some reason (and they would never reveal it) my fish were suspect. Perhaps they thought them unorthodox.

A true surf-caster is a man who loves the sea. Far beyond the prize of any great fish he might land, is the exhilaration of the waves. In the summer along the New Jersey coast they came in in sets of three, in great, racing combers. You could hear their dull booms far inland. Then there was the smell of the salt marsh. When the wind was off-shore these arching sea-horses raced in with long white manes streaming from their tips. From the marsh at sunset you heard the cry of shore-fowl. The haunting, space-hinting cry of the curlew; is there a more moving call by any sea? There were days of dull mist which blurred the headlands. Then a white fog, with the hot sun behind it, when the hissing surf shone like burnished silver. And then the long hot afternoons when the mirage came and the liners far off the yellow coast came past in streamers, or sailed upside down.

These are the things which fill the eye, and heart, and mind of the veteran surf-caster. These are often all that he brings home after a hard day's work, with the sandpipers dancing along the shore. Surf-casting is not a duffer's sport. And you are sure to catch many more fish from a boat.

GOING FISHING

For some reason, perhaps experience, we had the belief that the striped channel bass always struck best by night. There was a rod-maker along that coast who gave as a prize each year 'a handsome snakewood rod,' with German silver mounting, and agate guides, to the person who caught the biggest channel bass. One year the man who lived next door to me won it with a 42 pounder. He was very professional, having taken a house where he could command the sea, and having a glass case in that house full of green-heart, snakewood, and split-cane rods. Below the case was a chest of drawers containing Vom Hofe reels, Pfluegers, with ratchet and drag, and cast-off so that the spool could run free without turning the handle. Being an intensely religious man he never fished on Sundays; but that had nothing to do with 'practising.' So, when other people were at church, he and some of his old cronies would totter stiffly down to the beach and practise casting with just the sinker. For some reason—because of the ecstasy of it, I suppose—he seemed to get his strength back the minute he took his stance to make a cast.

It was a delight to watch the even parabola of his sinker, sailing surely to precisely where he had intended it. A back-lash, from him, would have been sacrilege. But there were other casters, among the summer lot, who were not so skilful. One summer day a novice, making the sweeping sidewise cast among a lot of enthusiasts at the end of our local wooden pier, rotated with all his might to shoot his sinker out to sea, but, unfortunately, caught a Japanese in the ear.

The hook was driven with such force that it pulled the ear forward and entered the Jap's skull. The lead sinker then swiftly spun around his head, and, *clunk!* hit him on the forehead and almost brained him.

But we, we locals, detested pier fishing. It meant a crowd; and that meant you lost the chief thing in surf-casting—the luxury of your own solitude. That, and trying to solve the sea—guessing whether this or that sand-bar had shifted—these things are the very essence of surf fishing. Then, to haul 2- or 3-lb. fish up like a bucket is an entirely different thing from beaching a fighting 25-pounder through heavy waves. There, every bit of your skill and intelligence is called upon. And quickly. In these conditions, with a heavy undertow and the last receding wave adding pounds to your line-pull, you can make a mistake only once.

Not able to play Sancho Panza to my revered neighbour, and feeling (quite correctly) that I had little chance of ever winning that fine prize rod myself, I attached myself to the next-best fisherman I knew along that stretch

Surf-casting is not a duffer's sport

of coast. He was an old ex-German. I did not know what his profession was, or his politics; nor did I care. All I knew was that if I did want to be in at the killing of one of these monster fish, he was the man for me. He felt likewise.

You cannot buy enthusiasm. Nor a small boy who will run a mile to fetch your bait. Or someone who will sit silent, for hours, while you ruminate. Someone who will eagerly hold your rod while you take a snooze. Or, even more wondrous companion, a boy who will collect driftwood for a fire on cold nights, when the driftwood burns green from the copper in it; and you two sit, avidly eating the bait—the fat clams you have roasted in the embers. Clams scorned by the channel bass.

But one moonlit night they did not scorn them. The German had waded far out and made his cast. Now he was drying himself by our fire. He had taken up all slack. With the click on, his rod was leaning over a 'Y' that he always brought along to rest it on—for these surf rods are not light things; if you can afford it, you use a heavy belt with a leather cup to hold the butt of your rod against you while you are fighting a fish. *And the reel screamed!*

I did not know a word of German then. But I heard a sputter of them. He was into a big fish. There was no doubt about that, the way the German's rod was bending—*and jerking*. Joe's bark showed that even he had realised this moment's significance. For the German nearly went crazy. What had happened was that he had jammed his reel. If my wealthy neighbour had reels with gadgets that made me envious, this German had tackle which made my heart ache. His reel not only had a drag, but super-super-drags. And one of them had 'frozen.' The spool was locked solid. The only thing to do now was run back and forth to the surf, or up and down the coast, *as the fish played him!*

In this unforeseen tug-of-war the fat German showed almost an indecent agility. One minute he would be shouting commands to me from atop the sand dunes (though what I could do about it, I could not see!); the next he would be racing past me towards the surf. The bass had made a run out for deep water. The fish had the upper hand for some time. 'Big von! Big von!' the German kept shouting at me. But the bend of his rod had already told me that. Finally loud Teuton yelps from the sand dunes announced that the German was beaching him.

And very skilfully he did it! Watching for an incoming wave, he went backwards with it. The fish was tired. The German got him just ahead of the wave and raced shorewards with it, keeping a taut line, bringing the fish with it as the wave surged far up the sands. Then he held it. The wave retreated. And there in the moonlight flapped a huge striped channel bass.

Then I broke the line.

I had tried to pull the fish farther upwards with it. Fatal ignorance! His dead weight snapped the Cuttyhunk forthwith. But I landed it. I ran down and fell upon it, thrusting my hand and arm well up through its gills. A scratchy gesture. But when the next wave came we were holding the prize up in the moonlight—just to look at it.

Every man has a fish in his life that haunts him; that particular big one which got away. Sometimes even I lie awake and groan at nights over an 8-lb. sea trout I had on for 2 hrs. and 40 mins. on a 3X leader up at Laxo in the Shetlands. It gets a pound bigger every time I tell about it. And how big that German's striped bass would have been, had the next wave carried it back, I cannot say. But when we went down into the town and woke up Mr. Seager (the rod maker) in the dead of night, so that he could weigh it while it was still wet, it pulled down the spring-scale to only 25½ lb. It did not qualify even among the first three that season. It won no prize. But it won an imperishable place in my memory, for it was the first *big* game fish that I had ever seen killed.

I still see the night, for it was by a flume, with the silent lighthouse on the other side; and in this flume we used to stand on the cross-beams and scoop up the herring, with dip nets, as they tried to rush the fall of peat-coloured water to get into Deal Lake. Our swift, sweeping dips, almost as fast as paddles, ended with a thud when a fish was in our net. We kids sold them around the town for three or four cents each. Then, in the spring, the small fish came out of the lake (probably spawned a couple of years back) about the size of large Marchand sardines. These we caught in masses and sold them for bait, or put some in jam jars and salted them down. (I know that herrings are supposed to spawn in the sea; and that their ova, in jelly-like masses, are alleged to sink to the bottom. Yet these were certainly herring that we caught going up that flume.) Always the same technique: the big hook was inserted through the mouth, out through a gill, then turned round and pulled through the fish again near the tail. On this triangular-swivel tackle the 3-ply leader always had a cork (just an ordinary bottle cork) split and closed over it, so that it could be slid along. By this means we adjusted

9

the ratio of the leader so that the hook could always float several inches clear from the bottom, which kept it away from crabs.

With these we caught weakfish, which, with their hundreds of spots and fine mouths, look like trout, and are actually called Bay Trout as you go southwards along the Atlantic coast, although they do not have the adipose fin. They have a fine, firm white flesh, are magnificent eating, and are one of the gamer sea fish.

We also used crabs for bait. The American crab sheds his shell, I think every year; and he does so in four stages. First he is a hard-shell; then a crack-shell—he is ready to shed; then a 'shedder.' With this last you may take the two sharp end tips, bend them back, and break him out. There he lies in your hand; the same colouring of dark green, with white and blue claws—but with the essential character that his skin is already so tough—ready to form the hard shell again—that he will stick on your hook; and, unless you are clumsy, stand any amount of casting. He is delicious to eat then; and 'Soft-Shell' American crabs, fried in sizzling fat and bread-crumbs, served with Tartar sauce, are a dish to delight any gourmet. These are another of the rewards of a surf-caster's life; for, in the long summer months the shallow salt lagoons are full of these soft-shell crabs, helpless objects, some of which you will see being carried along on the hard-shells' backs.

But to the surf-caster, there is probably nothing that can touch a run of 'bluies.' These are a fighting fish of the mackerel family which run in schools. You use a lead 'squid.' Viewed laterally, it is a sharp-edged, sharp-pointed object, made of lead, very like a double spear point. A cross-section of its centre would be a very sharp-pointed diamond. On one end of this is a heavy black hook. And so fiercely do the bluies strike that they will often snap this hook off. You use a wire trace, burnish the lead squid silver-bright with your knife each day before you use it; then you cast this, like a Devon or a Dowegiac, into the tide rip or patch of bay where you think the bluefish are schooling. With your big-spooled, quadruple reel you reel in the instant the squid hits the water. It darts toward you through the green sea like a flashing fish. When a bluie hits that your rod almost leaves your hands. It is always a battle to land him.

Then, on the great sweep of Barnegat Bay, we 'chummed' for bluies, sailing a cat-boat with the sheets fairly free, or one of those spoon-bowed sneak-boxes (which we used later duck shooting), towing astern a bag full of crushed-up menhaden—a herring-like fish, which stinks like hell, you think, because about the only other time you see it is when the New Jersey farmers are using it for fertiliser. These oily menhadens leave a broad streak of oil in the wake of your sailboat. The bluefish love menhadens. They come racing across the bay towards that tell-tale, promising oil streak—and there, darting through it, is your trolling 'squid.'

If you are alone in a sneak-box (it is only comfortable for two anyway) you will have your hands full with both sail and fish at the same time.

In the meantime, as the summer days go on, your skin becomes tanned like leather; your eyebrows turn white from salt and sun; and your hair becomes bleached white as a baby Swede's. Drying your line at night, walking along the balcony of the old wooden hotel which used to lie near Barnegat Light, you were so healthy, content, still thrumming with the day's sport, that you felt all this was too good to be true.

Well, it was. Lying there at nights during one of the vacations from my University, watching the beam of the Light, my ears filled with that satisfying sound of the ceaseless surf below me, I knew that my days of long leave would soon be ended. I would have to work pretty soon; the fishing-rods would be put away. Two weeks a year for my own self would be about the most I could hope for. And not these long golden summers.

But then there is the inland fishing, fresh-water, which brings with it other settings and an entirely different philosophy. I mean, by philosophy, the thoughts and meditations which come to you while you are fishing. For fresh-water thoughts have not the grandeur which comes from viewing the vast Atlantic. You must realise I am not talking now about fishing from piers and jetties, with other people, or even with buildings in sight of you; I speak of what the deep-dyed surf-caster always longs for—just the sea and himself.

And I exempt from this, of course, fishing for sea trout or salmon in the raw sweeps of romantic Scotland, or in the Hebrides, or the Shetlands, when the heather turns wine-red at sunset. No scenes could be grander than those.

But, otherwise, you may become contemplative until you are a very Izaak Walton under your willow tree, or have the grace to meet Nature with an open heart like Lord Grey of Fallodon; but, you must admit, your rewards will be less physically exhilarating. Your philosophical reflections may be—they are almost sure to be—more delicate, perhaps reach a finer perception—the salt sea jars you too much—but they are more on the contemplative than the active side.

We Americans have two fish, the small-mouth and the large-mouth bass, which have never received their proper recognition from fishermen of other countries. We used to think that they were the gamest fish, inch-for-inch and pound-for-pound, that swims. (Except a little fish called the 'bonefish' which you find in the shallows of the coral reefs off the Florida Keys.) I used to believe that—until I met the sea trout. Yet even now, inch-for-inch, pound-for-pound, I rather think it is a toss up.

The small-mouth is far and away the gamer of the two bass. To be at his best he ought to be in the cold, clear, spring-fed lakes of upper New York State, or some of the cold northern lakes, such as those in Wisconsin. When he strikes, if he hits a surface, or sub-surface bait, he will leap into the sky like Nijinsky, fighting on the surface all the time until you get him into the boat. And on each of these leaps your heart stops, for you know he is violently flicking his stubborn head, trying to shake out your lure.

For these fine fresh-water game fish you bait-cast. Here again you use the quadruple reel (one turn of the handle means four turns of the spool); and here again your intelligent thumb, ever so delicately braking, must control the spinning reel so that you do not get a back-lash. It is one-handed casting, with a rod seldom over six feet long, with a finely knit un-oiled silk line. This braided, unfinished silk line is the very acme of pliability. And, as I have said, your brains must be in your thumb.

You cast with 'plugs.' A surface bait like the Wilson Wobbler, a white-painted, cigar-shaped thing, with scarlet fluting; compact, painted Dowegiacs, which look like minnows—and even a white-painted float with a revolving head—which putters along the surface like a tug-boat; and the instant your plug hits the water you must start to reel it toward you. Nobody can prove exactly why the bass do strike at some of these lures—they can't think that white thing zig-zagging through the water is a *fish*. Nor with the Jamison Coaxer, a white, egg-shaped arrangement, with one hook fastened to another, paralleled by a scarlet feather. I myself think they strike from anger. For I have painted a clothes-pin red, cast it over their nests (when the male bass was patrolling them); and had them *wham* at it in perfect fury. Bass are also very fond of small grasshoppers and crickets.

I lived for years on a spring lake in the lower Catskills. I knew bass from the time I was 13 years old. And it was always a struggle, in the more infantile years, not to fish for bass over their nests. This rage of theirs was always their undoing. And here is an interesting thing: the bass (unless there was some freak of Nature that year) never came up to spawn until the temperature of these icy lakes had risen to 52 degrees Fahrenheit. Then, when they had made these round, whitish nests with their tails, the female had laid her eggs and the male had fertilised them with his milt, the female went off. It was always the male bass who was left to patrol the nest. He guarded it against other bass, or alligator-faced pike or pickerel.

These lakes turned blue in certain angles of the sun. They were cloaked in pine or beech or oak or chestnut. Their shores and their islands were grey granite rocks. It was a fine, hard scenery. There was nothing soft about the home of the small-mouth bass. In the autumn, with the turning leaves, these shores were a flame of red and yellow glory. You usually fished from a moving boat. You never anchored—not when you were bait-casting. When you cast your plug skilfully between some granite ledges—and had the fish carry it out of water with his leap—then you had one of the greatest thrills that fishing in the Americas can offer you.

The small-mouth has a hard, fighting mouth. He does not run as big as the large-mouth; a 4-lb. small-mouth, for example, would be considered very fine, almost an exceptional fish, certainly an unusual one, whereas a 4-lb. large-mouth is what we would call 'just middling.' A good fish, but nothing to brag about.

With the large-mouth, we had a style of fishing which was fascinating. I believe Leonard in New York now makes a special rod for it. It is split-cane, but short and stiff, like a stumpy trout rod. It is tough, because with this style of fishing, you have to strike with great force to drive the hook in. We used live small frogs.

I know it sounds inhumane. But a 'frog-fisher' always looks down on the man who uses the mechanical lures, sneering that he is 'fishing with machinery!' And to cast a live frog correctly required a skilled and gentle hand. For many years I fished with one of the finest 'frog casters' in the United States. At any rate, he made it almost a matter of course to win every prize given by the big sporting magazines.

But this doctor did not fish for prizes. He was a Southerner, from the Deep South, and a gentleman of the purest heart. He both looked and talked like the old President Theodore Roosevelt, who, he asserted, was what an all-round man should be. And, although he had just enough to keep him comfortable, this fine old doctor didn't care a whoop for either money, fame, even medical distinction; he lived the year round for just one month—July.

Every morning in July, except Sunday, a local man arrived at the doctor's door with 75 small, live frogs in a box. Then the doctor got into his old-fashioned car. Back he would come at sunset, red as a strawberry; and some dozen or so monster bass would be lying under a wet gunnysack. Where he got them from, such a continual supply of big ones, the neighbourhood never could make out. And then, too, the neighbours were not particularly interested; for, as I have said, this was in the money-making age, and most of the wealthy men who had their summer homes around that lake were merely tolerant of the doctor, liking him, but thinking him rather a fool—to go off fishing in the hot sun that way.

But he baited me so often about my 'fishing with machinery' that I took to frog-casting in sheer self-defence. I caught his fever.

There was a shallow, sandy-bottomed lake that it took us some hours to get to. A mite too slack, this reedy-marged expanse, for the vigorous small-mouth. There was a sort of back-bone of willows that seemed to grow almost out of the water along the centre of it.

'Negley,' the old doctor would say, baiting a fresh frog through its lips, 'the big old bass, the wise ones, lie under the shade of those willows in the heat of the day. Now there's one . . . just . . . there . . . that I've stirred once or twice . . .'

As he said 'just there' the doctor made his cast—plenty of line already stripped off the reel over the fingers of one hand; the *dressed* silk line, in this case, 'shooting' easily through the guides. The art is to cast your frog so that there is no jerk. You mustn't kill him, or take the life out of him, by jerking his head about. You must drop him gently *on the willows*.

'Y-e-e-s . . .' said the doctor, reminiscently; 'he must be at least five pounds . . . that fellow under there.'

And as he said that he was gently coaxing the frog off the willow branch into the water. The frog dropped. Instantly, it began to swim—with kicks. If the bass didn't take it then, the doctor pulled the line in, strip fashion, so that each pull straightened out the frog's legs, and each pause gave it time to kick again. But usually a big waiting bass was ready for it.

There was a swirl—and the swimming frog was taken under.

'But you don't strike now, Negley!'

14

No, the doctor explained; that would only mean that you pulled the frog out of the bass's mouth. 'Because these large-mouth always take a frog, first, sideways. Then they swim off and down a bit, blow it out, then take it in head-on!' So, while he was saying this, I watched with apprehensive stare the line sliding through the big guides of the Leonard rod. The doctor made no attempt to stop it; on the contrary, he was obediently paying it out—so that the bass should feel no pull.

Then there was a pause when the line stopped moving. The doctor's jaw muscles began to set. Then the line started slowly moving out again. Carefully, oh so carefully, the doctor gently took in all the slack; then he leaned back—*struck!*

Well, if you have ever stirred a paddle around in a bath tub, you can imagine the rumpus that was aroused. A huge bass—five, six, possibly eight pounds, had had the hook driven deep into him. He was wild. He came from the surface, the spray flying away from him, arched, turned like a fighting plane in a dog-fight—and crashed back into the water again.

'Away!' shouted the doctor; 'get me away from those willows! Work out into the lake! For God's sake—keep your side to him. Wait—don't move—he's making a run! Ah—got you, you beauty!'

The fish had flung out into the sunny air, crashed back again. And, in all these contradictory commands, I had won the valuable space between us and the shore. The art of frog-casting will make you dissatisfied with the artificial lures. Its drama is more visible, because you are watching your frog for most of the time—a thing you seldom get the chance of doing when you are fishing with a live minnow. Always, after the doctor and I had killed a few satisfactory fish, we would deliberately chance losing one merely for the opportunity of watching the bass handle the frog; they always did what the doctor said—took it from the side, then swam off and down to blow it out. You never came closer to watching a fish *thinking* than when you saw one of these deep-shouldered bass eye the frog . . . and bear down on it to swallow it head on. Then, when you struck, at these close distances, you witnessed all the frantic energy you had set in motion.

As to the cruelty of this sport, it cannot be any more unpardonable than baiting a live minnow through the back and letting the doomed thing swim. Sometimes the frogs would come back with their 'trousers' ripped off, or long triangular rips in their green and white skin; this meant that a pike or pickerel had taken a snatch at it, with their long rows of slanting teeth. We always killed these frogs immediately and threw them ashore. The doctor, too, had a sense of fair play, even with frogs; he never used one for more than four casts. 'Then he's served his time,' he would say with a smile, looking at me over the tops of his spectacles; 'he's a free frog.' So, when we pulled ashore under some shady tree for luncheon, the old man always released a dozen or so lively little ones. *His* gentle casting had not hurt them. A less-skilled man might kill the frog in two casts. And they would grow up, said the doctor, reminding me of Uncle Remus, to sing the booming bull-frog song: 'Doncher-believe-'um! Doncher-believe-'um!'

I have also often taken bass on a red fly like the Parmachenee Belle or the Cardinal.

These firm, fighting bass from the northern lakes had a fine white flesh which flaked easily when you prepared them cold, after boiling them. The doctor made a salad such as Prunier's in Paris would have been proud to list. He put the cold, flaked bass on ice and kept it over-night. In the morning his old Negro cook took some fresh lettuce and chopped it rather fine. Then the doctor made a mayonnaise, pungent with mustard. He put bass, lettuce, and plentiful mayonnaise in a bowl, stirred it round until it was homogeneous, like one of the famous lobster salads of Scott's; then he made a mould of it and put it back upon the ice again. At lunch on a hot day—and American summers are often more than tropical—this highly seasoned, cold bass salad could make even a dyspeptic a gourmand.

Further south the large-mouth bass reach an enormous size; I believe an 8-lb. bass is not at all an uncommon fish in Florida. But just as fish often take their colouring from the bottom, so does their flesh take its taste, both from their food—as, when Rainbow trout have plenty of crayfish to feed upon, which makes their flesh almost salmon-pink—and the temperature, speed, clarity of the water they live in. The lobster, for instance, improves along the American coast as you go up to Maine, living in the cold Greenland Current. Oysters are more succulent when dredged from northern waters. And, I feel sure, the quality of the American bass, both as a fighter and as a food, must deteriorate, as you catch him southward.

I know I took a risk when I opened this book with what the Englishman would call 'coarse fish.' We in the United States know no such distinction. In England it must be admitted that the salmon and trout are two fish supposed to be caught only by 'gentlemen.' You have a whole social order built upon it, proof of which is the 'fishing hotel.' Which of us has travelled the West Coast of Ireland, the Shetlands, the Outer Hebrides, or the West Country of Somerset and Devon, without knowing the grisly difference between the 'fishing,' or gentleman's hotel, and that dingy pub with the dirty linen catering for the 'commercials'? The point needs no more contention. Except one further point; to be recognised as a first-class fly fisherman in England means that you have won a definite position of merit. It is a distinction, and rightly so. That makes up for any amount of the snobbism with which you would bedeck this noble sport. Whereas, in the United States up to the end of the last war, a few men like Henry van Dyke might have gained some distinction, and Zane Grey with his kills of monster sea fish certainly won a world-wide notoriety, but it was chiefly because of their *writings* about it. Van Dyke with his fine philosophy; Zane Grey with his vivid sensationalism. In all the trout and salmon states we have fly-fishing clubs whose members, with both dry and wet-fly, are probably as good as the experts you will find in England. But for the *ordinary* citizen (and by that I mean a poor man), fishing was considered a waste of time, even a waster's avocation.

Oddly enough, golf was not.

But as one old river character said to me: 'Fishing makes you think.' There was not a town in the States which did not have its very sect of enthusiasts, with always a 'character,' very often the town drunk, whose solace was to sit idle days beside some stream, pond, lake, or even marsh, with a rod. The first drink I ever had in my life was from one of these. His name was 'Spieler' Welsh. Why the Spieler, I never knew; he neither talked much nor sang. Which last, God forbid! My mind rocks even now when I consider the prospect of that evil old man breaking into song. But Spieler was kind; and, managing to escape from my house, I went with him one misty night to where, perched on a bridge, we sat down to fish for catfish, with raw liver, where an ill-used little stream still went into a swamp. Spieler showed me how to slide my hand up their slippery sides from the tail—so that the back and two side spikes of their fins passed harmlessly up between my fingers— and then grip them, while, with the catfish 'gurking,' I twisted out the hook. A white-belly catfish can be a very toothsome dish; a bit sweet, like eel; 'Catfish & Waffles' were once a celebrated Philadelphia specialty in the inns along the Schuylkill.

Spieler, pleased with our catch, fished a flask of 'rot-gut' whiskey from his back pocket: 'Here, Kid—have some bait.' I obediently took a long pull—and nearly blew out a lung: it was, as the Indians correctly called it, fire-water!

Beginning with Spieler Welsh, on that misty moonlit night, fish lured me. I was even more drawn to them than they were to my baits. It is a deep pleasure today to walk beside some English stream, without a rod, and watch the trout, and wonder what they are doing, thinking, opening their little negro mouths as they lie in the food stream. I feel no impatience. I would watch any fish; they fascinate me—even on a fishmonger's plate.

And so, drawn by this lure, I fished in still ponds where the yellow water-lilies never moved in the heat of the day, and miasmic stretches of marshy water where the turtles dropped from the dead branches of fallen trees, *plop-plop-plop*, as your canoe came along; lonely stretches, safe from man, where the red-winged blackbirds sang and built their nests in tufts of reeds and the solitary blue heron stopped his broody fishing to flap away. All these settings said things to me. Then, as I have described, I mastered the art and joined the coterie of fanatic surf-casters; here was a great glory. And then the skill, and the thrills, of bait-casting. I loved them all. You will find no record fish in this book (except one). And then I stopped fishing.

I don't want this book to be any more autobiographical than it need be, but I show personal evidence to prove my point: the fact that, to a receptive person, what you get out of fishing is infinitely more than fish. For that reason I believe that neither size nor numbers should matter much; fishing should be the exercise of your skill—and its reward the spots it brings you to. If these are not your main objectives, then you don't know fishing. And so, feeling this way about it, I knew that when I deliberately gave up fishing for a time I was knuckling under to circumstances.

One day it occurred to me that the three things I knew and loved best—fishing, shooting, sailing—would never be any good to me. Or *for* me. They were all useless things; you could not make any money out of them. Indeed, I was wasting too much of that fleeting thing called Time upon them. If I kept on in this way I would come to no good. Had this not been prophesied? So, away with childish things; I had to get on!

Actually, a decision, as such, was never made; for, I thought, I had fallen in love. And imperceptibly I lost all interest in the other ones. Almost automatically, I hung the long greenheart surf rod by its tip from a nail; it is just one long rod with the detachable, cord-wrapped butt. The little steel Bristol bait-casting rod went into its cloth case in its four sections. An Abbey & Imbrie 'Duplex' bass and trout rod went into the velvet slots of its wooden case. The lines were dried and went away.

So did I. I sailed for England, a few days before the last war began. Six years later when I returned, still leather-tanned from Egypt's suns, I found the greenheart off the nail, lying *across* the cupboard, bent like a bow. It was finished. But the history of the other two rods is encouraging; for, in 1921-22 in British Columbia, both of them helped to keep me alive—at least, they kept me in cheap food. The trout rod was last used in 1929 trout fishing in the Caucasus, where its brittle tip broke. The bait-casting rod and the old, but very fine, Vom Hofe reel caught me many a fine trout in 1935 and 1936 in the Slovenian Alps, bait-casting Devons. Then it, too, broke. Hardy Bros., somewhere around 1930, when I returned from Russia, made me a copy of the Abbey & Imbrie 'Duplex,' with their own improvements (which you would expect from Hardy); and, as late as December 1940, I gave myself a Christmas present by having Hardy make me an American greenheart surf-casting rod. I am experimenting with it now on the coast of North Devon. You never know: even this fine rod might help to feed me some day.

But, in those early days, the other half of the fun of fishing was when you actually *had* to fish for food. It undoubtedly gives an added tang to it. I have fished for trout, frantically, in the still pools of the drying-up streams in West Virginia, when there was a drought on, and when your line, despite the care you had taken to crawl up on your belly to the stream, hit the still water like a clothes-line. I have fastened split buck-shot on a mosquito net, and dragged the pools for trout under such conditions. Such was our hunger. And I have 'stomped' suckers; gone along in the heat of the day in those tanbark mountains, banging rocks down on rocks which reached out, overhanging, to stun the fish that were sheltering from the blazing sun under them. Fishing for the pot, I have even gleefully gobbled carp that simply reeked of river mud.

This was cruising in an 18-foot gunning skiff down the Chesapeake Bay, where we slept ashore in a Baker shelter tent at nights, and did not stock up on food; first, because we had not the money; finally, because, lured by the promise of the famous Betterton perch, we had counted upon living off the fishing grounds. But there were no Betterton perch; I doubt if there ever have been any Betterton perch; I still think, angrily, that they were swimming only in the facile mind of the steamship company's advertising manager.

Lured to our destruction by pangs shockingly similar to real starvation, we shot blackbirds with our .22, put them in a 'D' net, and caught crabs with them. Have you ever tried to live on lukewarm crab-meat? No? Well, don't try it; it is thirty-one years ago now, almost to the July day on which I am writing this, yet I can still remember one dismal morning, with the mist lifting off the soggy bayou, when my young brother and another fellow and I heaved a pot of crabs we had been boiling overboard. We would die, we pledged ourselves, before we ate another crab!

Then, knowing that this brave resolve must be backed up by deeds and not words, we pushed up a river called the Sassafrass. Here I threaded some corn on a hook, and, lo! I caught a 12-lb. carp. We could not believe it when we got him ashore.

Being prudent, we decided we would not eat it all at one sitting. That night we cut some of it into steaks and broiled it across a little Arizona grid that was part of our compact camping kit. It was filthy. Still, it *was* food. So we wrapped the rest of it in a towel and put it in a pot over the fire embers to boil. And, sitting thus in the woods, with full stomachs for the first time in weeks, we fell asleep. The unaccustomed food had anaesthetised us.

When we woke in the morning the carp had disintegrated. So had the towel. And as we were unable to distinguish which was which we threw the whole mess back into the river again. We then tried gigging for fish at night with a trident, spearing everything we could bring under the beam of an acetylene bicycle lamp; but after I had shaken off four or five gar (a form of freshwater swordfish) back among the pyjama-clad legs of the other two, we gave this up in despair.

We robbed orchards, crops, melon patches, even a store, before letters came bringing money from our frightened people. No letters more poignant than ours to them have ever been sent.

And so those years passed.

There are a few memories which still stand out from them. One was a night when in an $11\frac{1}{2}$-ton yawl we anchored in a place called Deep Harbour,

Maryland. At sunset Joe and I (he was killed at Château Thierry) got out our shotguns and took the dinghy ashore to go after some snipe we saw feeding along the waterline. We got three, and they were the treat of that night's dinner. After dinner, with the water lapping gently against our sides, and with a full moon rising, we lazily fished for catfish. Although we were hard up for any kind of food then, we did not care whether we caught any or not; the night was so beautiful. We were hushed by it. I was not writing in those days, except to amuse myself; but I wanted so much to put the enchantment of that night into words that it hurt. And then as we were sitting there, not talking, a hound bayed far up on the hill . . . a hound baying at the moon. I shall always remember that.

Then—last of the long, golden summers—was the final cruise of the *Polecat*. She was a 25-foot, clinker-built, *condemned* Government naval cutter. She was bought by the 'Captain' of my father's yacht for $4—and I don't think she was worth it. They say you can't caulk a clinker-built boat; but Carmen, who had pulled her ashore to live in her during the winter, poured hot tar in her seams. He did this to keep the wind out.

This is a fishing and not a sailing book; but it is about Things in the Water—and about the most wicked thing *I* have ever seen in the water was the old *Polecat*. She 'worked'; her sides opened and shut like an accordion; she threatened to take you to the bottom at any minute. She wasn't safe because you could neither beach her (she was too heavy for that) nor lie off-shore. The compromise was to find some creek or shelter of land at night, bale her dry at midnight, set the alarm clock for 7 a.m., and then pray that you would wake up in time. First thing every morning we baled her dry again. And it was running into one of these creeks far down the Delaware Bay, where the New Jersey marshes stretch an unbroken forty miles inland—and you can see the sails over in the Maurice River, working into Bivalve, New Jersey, fifteen miles across the flat marsh—that we encountered the 'Catty-rackers.'

'Cattyrackers' are peculiar to the Delaware Bay. They are the refuse of the oyster fleet. In the Delaware Bay you may plant seed oysters with an engine; but you must dredge with sail. This is in the 'R' months—and a large part of the Delaware Bay, especially the shoal oyster-waters around Maurice River Cove, freezes over in the winter. Even if it doesn't, the blocks and standing gear get sheeted with ice. This has to be broken, or chopped away. Fingers go in the process, sometimes a leg. The result is that you have these human derelicts, remnants, incapacitated either from the ice—or drink.

If you put together these four 'cattyrackers' we found in the *Travelling Sam*, you might have had a four-headed monster, but you would still not have had a complete man. Outstanding among them was their leader, a man with a peg-leg; and their cookie, a mean little runt with one eye. They were hauling a seine across the sand-shoals off Oyster Gut, catching bay trout, eels, flounders, horse-shoe crabs, anything that could not get through their fine (and illegal) mesh. They threw the horse-shoe crabs they caught into a corral they had built, to die, rot, smell to heaven, and eventually be sold as fertiliser to the farmers on the mainland behind the marsh. The fresh fish they sold at a little town named Fortescue about five miles up on a strip of solid sand. A catch sold, they bought the minimum of food to keep them alive—the rest went on flasks of 'rot-gut whiskey.' That's 'cattyracking.'

We ran into the Gut at sunset and laid up beside the *Travelling Sam* because we were getting out of a storm, but especially because we wanted some fresh oysters to make fritters. The Gut was not named Oyster for nothing; for, if you put on a pair of tennis shoes and waded up it at low tide, you could pick the little milk oysters off the rocks. We filled a gunnysack with them. With a can of sweet corn, flour, a couple of eggs and some condensed milk, they produced fritters that would have made M. Boulestin weep.

There was a fine, nice, rotten smell about that interminable stretch of salt marsh. A smell you would never forget, nor would you want to; there was a strong call of the untrammelled about it. And it was a splendid life to be young and living on the edge of it. We got up with the dawn, when the eastern sky was flaming in all its colours, and waded out into the salt water to help the dissolute cattyrackers haul their seine. The marsh was still at that hour, mute. The water in the bay was blackish green. The air was almost unbearably fresh. The cattyrackers would always give us any fish we wanted, letting us take our pick. There was triumph in it. So when the cattyrackers pushed off in their skiff to reach Fortescue before it woke, we sat down in the cockpit to a breakfast, cooked on the *Polecat's* ordinary kitchen range, of fried bay trout, buckwheat cakes, and mugs of steaming coffee. After which the cigarettes, forbidden at home, were nectar.

Life, we felt (and quite correctly), could not hold much more. There was always work about the boat, which gave us the satisfaction that we were 'doing something.' And there was always this surf-casting into the lovely bay. It is about thirty-five miles wide at that point. The cattyrackers were interested in the spectacle of surf-casting; but they could never understand the thrill I got out of playing a big bay trout: 'Why the hell don't you just haul him in?' they asked. And when I replied that he would break my line, they countered: 'Hell—you-all can buy a *thicker* one, can't you?'

But the cattyrackers were not speaking to each other when we came on them. They had just fallen out over one of the most shocking marine adventures I had ever heard. They had been running the *Travelling Sam* as a speakeasy and gambling den. Their 'racket' was that the 'sports' of the town could come down to their boat at any time and buy bootleg whiskey by the glass. Also, if they felt inclined, they could have a little game. Stud poker. The poker game was probably on the level, because none of the *Travelling Sam* outfit could have had brains enough to cheat. But their trick was, and they had to bribe the local police to get it to work, to have the police raid the *Travelling Sam* (at a signal) whenever there came a night when the play was high—and there was a lot of 'big money' on the table.

When the raiding police banged on the door (for this was a house-boat), and the 'sports' vanished in all directions, then this outfit split the deserted money with the police and the *Travelling Sam* hurriedly moved on. They could never, of course, return to the same town. EVER ONWARDS was the motto of the *Travelling Sam*.

She was nothing but a hut built upon a float, with a door at either end. At their last town, when the police made their terrifying raid, one of the prominent citizens of that town panicked, and was fished out of the river about three miles down. This had scared the crew of the *Travelling Sam* into trying to earn an honest living. Which, they asserted, was a damn fool way of doing it. It meant hard work. So they had begun their life at Oyster Gut in an already disgruntled mood. Then came their adventure.

They had a rickety launch with which they used to tow the *Travelling Sam* from place to place. They had decided to take one more risk, try to run their poker game over at Bivalve, New Jersey. A bold resolve, for the crews of the oyster boats are furious fighters. On this trip old Peg-Leg declared that he would remain in the *Travelling Sam*, and not go in their launch. The other three could try to make that something engine go. But—the Delaware is a stormy bay. Treacherous. A sea gale, coming in against the swift ebb tide, instantly churns the surface into mountains.

The tow rope of the *Travelling Sam* parted.

'Now there was old Bill,' said One Eye, 'a-rompin' around like a bird in a cage. We dasn't go *near* him; it'd smash our launch to bits! Bill oughter known that!'

Peg-Leg said nothing.

'So . . . thar he was. . . .' One Eye and the others took turns vividly describing how one-legged Bill hopped from door to door, from window to window, as the *Travelling Sam* rotated like a slow merry-go-round in the stormy sea. Bill was yelling at them, telling them what he thought of them. A lot of yellow-bellies was the gist of it. One time he took their shotgun and fired at them. But *that* unfriendly act only drove them farther off.

Night fell; and down between Cape May and Lewes, Delaware, where the whole eighty miles of open bay races out through a narrow mouth, Bill went out on the roaring tide.

'It warn't no use to follow him.'

'And then what?' I asked.

Peg-Leg spat on the stove, watched it sizzle, and stared at me. He spat again, a better shot, which directly hit the grate.

'Yes—what?'

One Eye began to giggle. Then the other three lay back and howled. 'Pardner! if it ain't the God's truth I'll eat my foot. Bill come floatin' back in the mornin'. Yessir, sure as we're sittin' here, old Bill he come back. Floatin' back on the flood-tide just as pretty as Pharaoh's baby. Ain't that right, Bill? You did come back, didn't you? An' *didn't* we come out to git you? . . . just as if we was pickin' up a dead duck! Tell 'im, Bill.'

Bill told me. Then he glared at his comrades; he threatened them.

'I'm going to find me a woman. Not a *decent* woman. I'm a-going to find one of the most no-account women you can pick up along this bay. And I'm gonna *marry* her. You skunks don't appreciate me. But a woman like that— one what's been through the mill—*she* knows a good man when she gets one.'

This bit of rude philosophy amused me frequently in after years, particularly in post-war Paris; very often for its truth. I wondered at times what old Bill would have made of the Naughty 'Twenties in London. When I thought of him I longed for the dank, rank smell of that old salt marsh again.

I longed for the simplicity, and the sense of security that, somehow, it gave you. There, with a boat, a shotgun and a couple of rods, you could have a far fuller life than I was finding in the cities of Europe. Old Bill had a better existence than he knew; I had seen enough to know that. I had always suspected it; but now I *knew* it.

I was not the only one. When I returned to the States, a couple of years after the war had ended, I found that a dramatic change had taken place in the sense of values. The former 'useless' sports were no longer looked down upon. And the obligation to *make money* had lost some of its crippling effect. Perhaps it was the cynicism of our troops, returning to listen to the loud-mouthed orators; more likely it was the lives they saw in Europe—lives not altogether devoted to the money urge, but I found that the bloodless, pro-fessionally Puritanical men who had previously dominated our lives, forcing us because of their own parched spans to believe that the making of money was man's noblest effort, had gone. At least, their voices were no longer in command of the community.

An exhilarating urge for sport surged throughout the States. Golf clubs mushroomed into growth around the perimeter of all our big towns and cities. Marconi rigs sped like clouds of butterflies down Long Island Sound. There was a tremendous spurt in fishing reel and rod design—some of the latter quite awful. This *was* machinery! A truck driver I spoke with in Chicago, a Swede who could hardly yet talk American, boasted to me how he had just bought a tiny lake on the instalment plan over the border in Wis-consin: 'And dot damn lake is yust full of bass!' And then, of course, the inevitable began to happen; we began to get like England—sailing, shooting, even fishing were fast becoming a rich man's pleasure.

Shooting duck down on a 'pug hole' in the Illinois River bottoms, where the great southward flight funnels down from Canada (and where there was at least one 'Duck Club' with a £1,000 initiation fee), I complained to the local farmer whose marsh we had rented that there were, it seemed, about four men—who had to be paid something—between me and every duck.

'Wal, I'll tell 'e,' he drawled, spitting some tobacco juice, then scratch-ing the back of his chicken-like neck; 'it's like this—duck shootin's a luxor!'

That was the irony of it; duck shooting had become a luxury—just when the fog had cleared from our sense of values. Wherever it was at all possible, some money-making hound was buying up every bit of *controllable* fishing.

The thing seemed to be happening overnight! There seemed hardly a foot of the marshes I once knew as merely scorned wasteland that you could put your foot upon without trespass. Down in Currituck Sound, North Carolina, I found that the shooting or fishing rights over every foot of shoreline was owned by somebody, often a syndicate. The fine new game laws, which appeared under Roosevelt, divide the United States into three zones—Northern, Central and Southern—for ducks, brant, and geese; and at first you might shoot for a month only in either one of them. This gave the ducks a chance to get by. Moreover, you might not shoot until an hour after sunrise or after an hour before sunset; this prohibited the murderous shooting at the dawn or evening flights. You might not build a blind more than a certain number of yards out from shore; and you might no longer use live decoys. You were allowed only ten ducks and four geese a day.

All of which is almost too good to be true; but it has its reverse side. Shooting one day down on Currituck, a day so windy that only the pintails were up, I got my limit before 10 a.m. The geese were not coming near us; they were going down along the far strip of sand between the Sound and the Atlantic, flying high, their cry 'A-oook! A-oook!' coming to us faintly.

I aimed at an occasional duck that came whistling by, just for practice—until the local man with me in our boat behind the reed-blind could stand it no longer.

'Shoot 'em!' he cried; '*shoot 'em*—Andy Mellon don't own *all* those damn ducks!'

Andrew Mellon was the president of a big duck club that had just bought up a large stretch of marsh, both here and, I think, over in Albemarle Sound. These local Carolinians hated him for it.

'Why,' I said, 'do *you* people shoot more than your limit?'

He gave me a vulgar wink (he was half Indian) and pointed to a string of white swan flying innocently over our heads. 'Everything!' he said emphatically. 'Ever eat swan? Mister, we shoot every damn thing we can get—yes, and we "lamp" 'em at nights!'

He was malignant about it. Now that duck shooting had become fashionable, and rich men were buying up all the access to it, these local people felt they were being cheated. They would shoot any or everything, just to show they were not going to be done out of things. It was an ugly predicament for both the ducks, the fish, and the men who genuinely loved these sports. I

You are allowed only ten ducks and four geese a day

write this here, in this section about the States, because Roosevelt's wise Administration is bringing back the ducks to the States and Canada so that the great autumn flights will once again darken the skies. The breeding stock of waterfowl is estimated now to number almost four times what it was at the low point in 1932. As the supply of ducks has increased, the drastic laws have been relaxed. The fish, too, the bass, trout, and salmon, are also being rigorously protected and propagated. Reforestation will return their waters to them. And in the great national and local effort the democratic ideal of free fishing and shooting for all who love it is fast gaining headway. If this succeeds, with our new sense of values, the United States may once again become the sportsman's paradise. It is just possible.

II

*Russian Revolution—and Leonid Andriev's yellow perch; a voluntary exile
in British Columbia; the lonely house-boat; and keeping
yourself alive with rod and gun*

I have once seen fishing solace a very intelligent man. This was Leonid
Andriev, the Russian writer. It was in the spring of 1917, after the Kerensky
revolution, on the shallow Gulf of Finland. A few communistic Finns, with
their flat black hats, were still sitting in circles in the pine woods behind us,
making up their minds whether they were going to kill us or not; and, under
these conditions, I read Andriev's *The Red Laugh*—and understood every word
of it. I fished beside him at the mouth of the Chorney Retchka, the Black
River. Food was hard to come by; white bread was as rare a treat as cake;
meat was almost unobtainable. But there were fish.

In that shallow, glistening gulf, where you could walk out for hundreds
of yards, I caught a little sticklebackish fish which we cooked in a sort of
aspic. I set trot-lines for them at night. But it took about a hundred of them
to make a meal for the nest of us who lived in that wooden *datcha*. I was
jeeringly called upon to put my skill to the test.

And so I met Andriev, sitting moodily in his skiff, with a tame Finn, while the guns still barked in Kronstadt across the water—for there was still an unfinished internecine struggle being decided there. Andriev stared at it across the gulf and shook his head. 'Someone has let the sheep out of the stable,' he said to me; 'but who will ever put them back again!'

Then he stared moodily at his float. In a few seconds the creases in his forehead would smooth out. I watched him, day after day, when we knew that everything material we owned in the world was being taken away from us. Soon we might, in all truth, have nothing but this fishing left. And then one day he gave a shout, a scream; he had jumped up in his boat and was waving an arm. I rowed over.

Andriev had caught a 2-lb. yellow perch.

The internationality of the yellow perch is almost unbelievable. Like that travelled bird, the little tern, they seem to be found all over the world. Similarly, I caught a couple of pike (one of 10 lb.) strip-casting for them among the islands behind Stockholm. And in Egypt, behind Alexandria's breakwater, I trolled white chicken feathers with a strip of brass, for the ubiquitous mackerel.

But this was all the fishing I did until the World War was over.

In 1921 bad luck, by good fortune, drove me from Chicago to live in the forests of Canada. I picked a fairly uninhabited lake in the heart of Vancouver Island. And there, for two years, I hardly ever took my rods apart. They were in constant use.

They had to be, for I was just married, and very hard up. We needed any kind of free food we could get. For many months of the year trout were our staple diet, and I do not remember ever getting tired of either catching or eating them.

When I was carrying our stuff down from the clap-board store to the river pool I was startled by the sight of some twenty salmon passing up the stream. I could hardly believe I had come to such a paradise. But it was false; for, when I stood on the end of the plank pier and watched them, I saw they were all far-gone with spawning. Even more lamentable, they were covered with white sores. A red-eyed dog salmon passing sullenly up had his jaws crossed like a scissor-bill's. It was then that I learned that all the Pacific salmon spawn only once and then die. Literally, the hundreds, the thousands of passing-up salmon that I watched in that and the succeeding weeks were a

Red Host, come home to die. They were fighting their way up the river, then up the long twenty-mile lake, to the same stream, perhaps the same bed, where they had first been an egg either two or four years before.

Once you have seen that drama of the Pacific slope you will never forget it. These weary, doomed fish will haunt your memory. You will never become reconciled to the uncanny unreasonableness of it all. What law of nature willed it that millions upon millions of these fine fish should rot to death every year? When the streams diminish and the lake falls in the autumn, just before the rainy season, the putrefying bodies of these fish lie on the banks, or are caught in bushes, and the air reeks. That, too, you will never forget. Nor will you want to; for this sweet-sour reek brings back with it the sweep of those great primeval forests, water so clear that you sometimes think your skiff must be floating in air, and, of course, the feeling of being there when the world was freshly made—as you always do feel in the remote regions of British Columbia.

Settling down, eyeing rods, rifle and shotgun—plus a very overworked typewriter—I knew that these things would have to help considerably in keeping myself and my wife alive. They dare not fail me. For I have never been quite so broke in all my life. If the rod and my gun did not provide sufficient 'free' food, and if the typewriter did not produce paying short stories, then my wife and I would have to quit the country. Having seen it, having settled down for the first winter in a log house ashore, we made up our minds that that was just the one thing we would never do. And (it is not at all strange, when you come to think of it), I have never felt so *secure* in my life. My life was in my own hands. I called nobody master.

The lake had a 'waist' about half way up, where a pine-clad arm of bald granite mountain jutted out to form a narrows. In the upper ten miles of lake lived nobody, except the inhabitants of one logging camp at its far end, then engaged in cutting down ruthlessly one of the finest stands of virgin cedar left in the world. On our side of the lake the whole twenty miles of shoreline held just three residents: a professional cougar hunter (and bootlegger) down by the rickety wood bridge at the foot of the lake, where it began to spill over to form a rapid-white river that raced thirty miles down the mountains to the sea; and an old Irish doctor and his wife, who went down from the lake in the winter. Along this shore also lived a nomadic Englishman, honorary gamewarden, who moored his tiny house-boat wherever the whim moved him. And here I, too, securing one of these unpainted board shacks built upon a cedar raft, began a nomadic life that lasted two years.

There was a colony of 'house-boaters,' four or five in all, moored in the river pool below the bluff on which stood the one store at the foot of the lake; and, going uplake on that side, you passed nothing until you came to a startling, red-painted 'schloss,' built by a German self-exile; then the house-boat of Old Louis, the trapper; then after a couple of miles you came to a fine, shingled 'ranch house,' built by an English aristocrat; across some wasteland from him hibernated a Scotch hermit; a mile above him was the old log house of the original settler; then—nothing for ten miles until you reached the raw logging camp. It was not a crowded country.

These mixed loggers were Scandinavians, English 'remittance men,' Americans, even Sikhs. There were astonishingly few Canadians among them. They had no morals when it came to fish. Fish were just fish; catch them anyway you could. The nearest they came to a sporting effort was when they fished with preserved salmon eggs for bait (then illegal) over the potato peelings thrown overside by the flunkeys from the cook-house. The reason for using the potato peel to catch trout was visibility; if you sat on the edge of the raft on which floated the cook-house, you could look down at these potato peelings on the bottom—they nearly always fell white side up—and see the trout coming for your hook. Their greenish-dark backs, almost invisible against the green moss at the bottom, came across these white strips with almost a murderous intention. So they always appeared to us; for they were fine trout, deep-shouldered, with small heads, in perfect condition.

Most of them were Rainbows. But then there was the famous 'Cutthroat,' with the red by his gills, which could always be depended upon. The Rainbows would vanish when the lake got too warm in summer, and also during the winter months. They of the fine pink flesh. There were, also, Dolly Vardons; the gay, beautifully spotted, but slimy Char. These you caught only by deep fishing. I was a year on the lake before I ever knew they were there! I knew two Swedes, fishing with a salt-bag full of mashed salmon eggs —sunk to the bottom—who caught, lured by the blue oily discolouring made by those eggs, seventy-five of these mixed trout in one day. A murderous performance, because the British Columbia logger wants to eat neither trout nor salmon; he demands bacon and eggs and stacks upon stacks of hot-cakes. Or steak.

I felt poverty-stricken after a meal or two up at that big logging camp. They were irresistibly hospitable. And when, a bit bored with my own stretch, I went into the upper lake for ducks or trout, or both, they always insisted: 'Stop over and have a meal, Mister!' I always did. They were not scornful of either fly or spoon—they knew too much—but they did insist on improvements. One of these was the 'flasher.'

The 'flasher' is an ordinary shallow tin pie-plate, burnished bright, fixed on your line some forty feet ahead of your spoon. You troll it behind your boat as you row four or five, even ten miles down to the store. It gives you something to think about. 'It's sort of *advertising* for fish! Pardner,' said a logger. 'You see, in the heat of summer, these here doggone trout go down to the bottom—where it's cool. *Nothing* will bring 'em up. Won't even look at a salmon egg when they're down there, they're so damned lazy . . . *but use a "flasher," Pardner!* Yes siree—that fetches 'em!'

What happens is that a deep-lying trout, seeing this tin flashing in the water above him, comes up to investigate. He sees the 'flasher,' probably sheers off—but almost immediately after that he sees your spoon coming towards him flashing like a live fish—with its seductive row of coral beads.

'Yep!—when he sees that—he's done! I think it's the red that gets 'em—them beads. Or the red on the under side of your spoon. Makes 'em angry, maybe. But they hit it. First of all, of course, you got to *attract* 'em—understand?—that's where the little old "flasher" comes in. Pardner, the "flasher" is a killer!'

I've never used a 'flasher' (although I must say that I have wanted to on hungry occasions); but once in a while I would bring my skiff up to the log raft of the 'Push,' the foreman of the logging camp, with a couple of trout lying on the floorboards which even he would admit were not altogether without merit.

Across the lake, on the long stretch of uninhabited shore—where a herd of wild elk nibbled the underbrush—was one of the finest Rainbow creeks on the entire Pacific coast. I've seen them lying along the edge of the big slide of granite boulders at its mouth, rocks washed down by centuries of spring freshets, when they were packed tight as mackerel on a fishmonger's marble slab. Huge fish, with a six-pounder not at all an uncommon sight among them. It was a sight to drive you crazy. For if the riffle was not just right, blowing gently up into the mouth of the creek, they would not look at a fly.

I've camped in a pup-tent for four days among the grey boulders of its fan-like mouth, been rewarded by nothing but the rustling of deer or bear or elk in the woods at night, listened to the child-like cry of a cougar, and never stirred a fish. Then, when the riffle did come, I have had fishing such as I have never seen the like of anywhere before or since—except in lower Chile.

It was off this British Columbia creek that I learned what an extraordinary difference there can be—to some trout—between a Jock Scott and a Silver Doctor. They look very much alike to us; and *size* did not enter into this demonstration, because I had several Jock Scotts of exactly the same number as the Silver Doctor I lost. But with the Silver Doctor I had already landed three fine Rainbows, the largest being close to 4 lb., when a big brute of some six pounds or so took me straight under a sunken tree-root that had been washed down with the spring freshets. In that apple-green, clear water I could see him all the time. With my light rod (it was the old Abbey & Imbrie) I could not stop him. The cast broke. He jumped once—and was gone.

After which, that same morning, I never rose another fish. I took the Jock Scott as being the next-nearest fly and fished over dozens of big Rainbows I could see lying along the rim of the deep slant of grey rocks going down into the green water. Had they gone off for some reason? I would have thought so to this day, were it not for the unusual appearance of a launch that came up lake about two hours after I had started fishing. In it was the British Admiral commanding the China Station, who, stopping off at Victoria, had come up to the lake to try this famous Rainbow creek. A marten-trapper brought him up. He asked me what I was using, and I told him I had had some luck with a Silver Doctor. He put one on; and after a few casts he was into a big fish. I tried every fly I had in the book before I finally rowed off in disgust. Meanwhile I had watched him catch four or five big fish. His eyes were on the fish; he did not see me go; and he was in too much of a fever of expert fly-casting for me to interrupt him—and borrow a Silver Doctor.

I would have other days.

There was a sheltered little bay a short walk through the woods from the log bungalow where I lived that first winter. There was still time enough that autumn for me to catch some very fine trout there. In the States, in the Allegheny Mountains, I had always found fishing best at the sunset rise. There was a hatch of fly then, and trout were breaking all over the stretch of water

It was always a battle if they made for the reeds

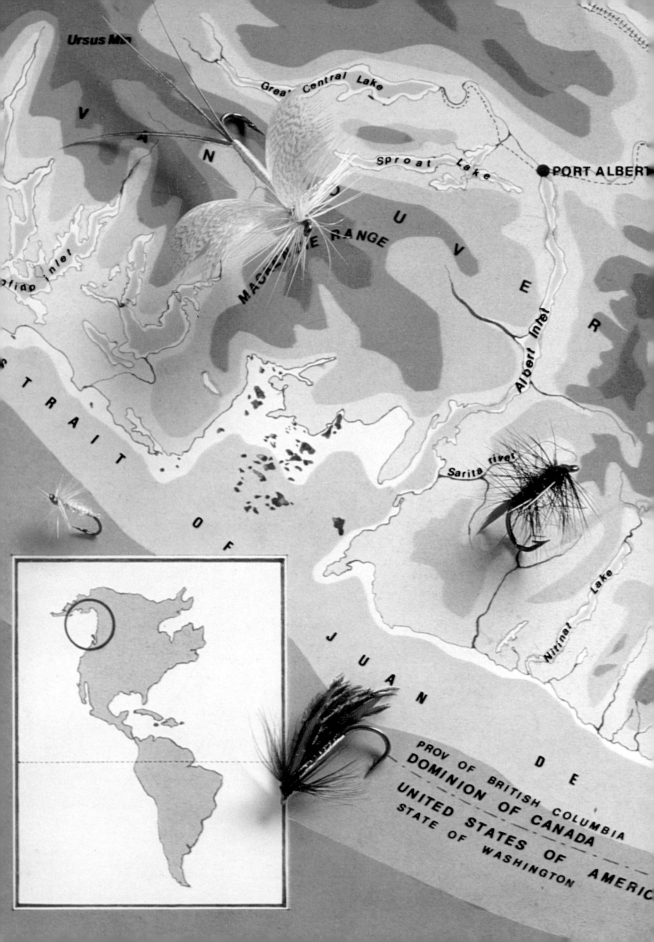

Ursus Mar

Great Central Lake

Sproat Lake

PORT ALBERN

VANCOUVER

MACKENZIE RANGE

ISLAND

Alberni Inlet

STRAIT

inlet

OF

JUAN

DE

Sarita river

Nitinat Lake

PROV OF BRITISH COLUMBIA
DOMINION OF CANADA
UNITED STATES OF AMERIC
STATE OF WASHINGTON

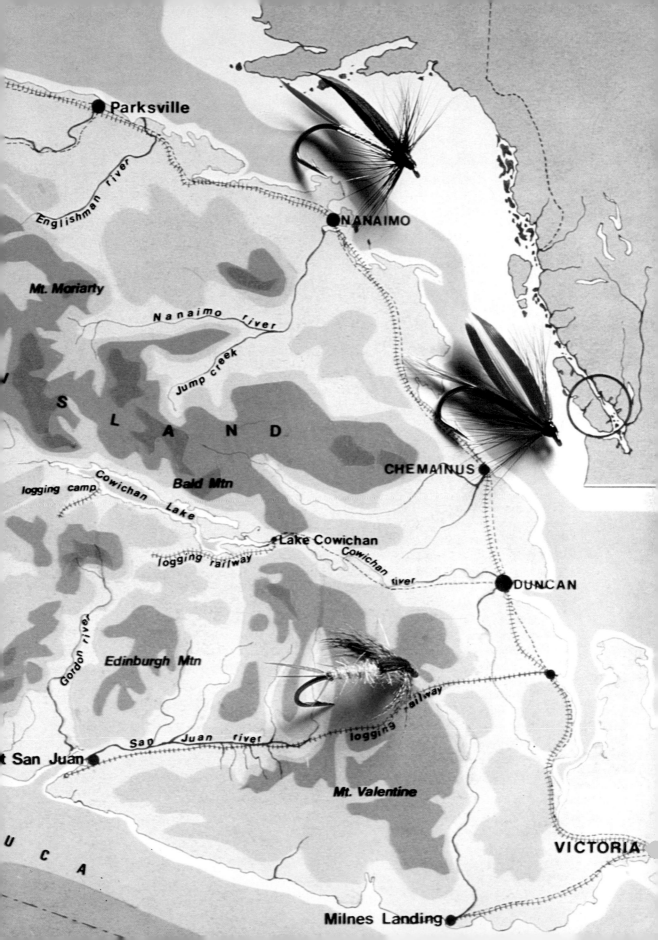

I knew best. I would fish till darkness, sometimes until long after. It was not unnatural, therefore, that first autumn in British Columbia, that I hardly ever fished for trout before the close of the day. I was slow in getting on to the psychology and the habits of the British Columbia trout—but it gave me some wonderful sunsets!

There was a rim of stiff reeds along one shore, the shore toward the west. Lying some distance off it, I could get plenty of enjoyment making a careful cast to the edge of the reeds. Sometimes there was too little wind (it so often fell with sunset); but that only made any trout I got all the more pleasurable. I could usually pick up one or two for dinner. It was always a battle, if they made for the reeds. It makes me smile to remember it now, for I never once thought of fishing in the open stretch of the little bay behind me. Next spring I found it stiff with trout!

But on those sunsets I was usually caught and held by the changing colours of the lake up beyond me. It seemed to fuse with the sun. The broad path of gleaming, burnished water. The shores dissolving into a pastel blue haze. The mountains at the far end of the lake turning into a powder of rose and lavender. The rock mountains seemed as nebulous as dust clouds. I was always caught by the wonder of it: I was literally 'spell-bound.' And when a trout jumped then, between me and the sun, the drops he shook off were golden.

With so much trout to be had we were prodigal with our cooking. Our favourite way, with the ones around two pounds, was to fillet them. These fillets we fried in breadcrumbs. My wife, who makes a nice, stiff mayonnaise sauce, contended that I always ate the fish for the mayonnaise. So I did. So I do, even here in London; salmon trout, with *sauce verte*, or salmon with *sauce tartare*. We might have been both broke and primitive in our log cabin in British Columbia; but fillets of Rainbow trout with *sauce mayonnaise* we had at least once a week in the days when trout were on.

I wish you could have seen the effect of these on Swanson, the huge Swedish hand-logger. 'Yennerally,' he said, sliding down almost a whole fillet, 'I don't eat trout—I yust catch 'em. Yust another little piece, thank you!'

Another way with, say, a 2½-pounder, was to make a stuffing of bread-crumbs, herbs, egg, and butter—tie its stomach up, when filled with this, with a bit of old line—then *bake* it in butter in the oven. When that was done we cut the line, the crisp skin peeled off the pink flesh, and there was one of the most delectably seasoned fish in the world.

Mere frying of them we reserved for quick meals like a breakfast, and there were long periods, at the beginning of the season, when I loved to eat my fill of those that we had boiled the previous night cold for breakfast. In some ways, I think that simple style was the best one of them all. The only seasoning then was salt.

You could never tire of this firm, pink flesh.

The old German across the lake had a bitter experience with his first spent salmon. He found two, perfectly good fish (he thought), lying dead on the bank. He took them as a present to Old Louis, the French-Canadian trapper. This was on the eve of the last war, and Old Louis, besides being deaf, and able neither to read nor write, hated Germans. He did not like his neighbour, though he had never said so. On this day, to his astonishment, Old Louis saw the German coming down the bank-path to his house-boat, bearing two definitely dead, spent, useless salmon—and the German handed him one of them! Old Louis seized it by the tail, made a full swing with it and knocked the German flat. It was a 10-lb. Cohoe.

The poor German had a mystery about him that gave him, it seemed, a secret satisfaction and yet made it inexpedient for him ever to return to Germany. Only one thing was known definitely: he had been an officer in a regular German regiment, long before the last war, in East Africa. His imitation Bavarian schloss that he had erected in the woods of British Columbia was full of the heads of African game. He had a story about every one of them, most of them interesting. He was a gentleman. He had some money sent out from Germany, enough in pre-war days for him to be wealthy on that lake. When the mark broke he became a pauper. He had nothing but his rifles and shotgun, for which he could not afford to buy ammunition, and a wife. In devious ways, mostly by doing sewing for the other settlers' wives, she kept them alive. And it was she who accepted a salmon from me with cries of joy.

Her gratitude made me feel cheap. This salmon was not too far gone to eat. I didn't fancy him. But I did eat another I had caught at the same time which seemed in about the same condition. I ate that one out of pride more than anything else, for it was the first salmon I had caught in British Columbia. I had been watching a dozen or so of them in the pool, down at the foot of the lake, while I was waiting for my weekly mail; there were several of them without any scars on them, which made them seem fairly fresh-run; so I took the short bait-casting rod with which I had been trolling a spoon as I rowed down the lake, hoping for a cutthroat trout, and put on a round-barrelled brass minnow. They say a British Columbia salmon never feeds when he is on his way up the swift rivers to the spawning beds. Maybe so. I cast again and again through these salmon that were resting temporarily in the pool; I'll admit they never looked at it; then this one switched his head round and snapped at it like a dog. He was 10 lb., and he gave me quite a fight, breaking as he did at once for the white water. His flesh felt firm as I unhooked him, and he was not too unpleasant to eat, although his flesh had already begun to lose its pink colour as the oil was being drained from it in the reproductive process. I think this one struck at my minnow from sheer rage.

But in the hope that I might pick up a trout, which would be something real to eat, I dropped this salmon at my cabin as I went past, and went on up the lake to the other side where there was a small off-lake, with a river running into it. Here I trolled across the mouth several times about an hour before sunset. This was a gloomy corner; no open vista of coloured sunset here, just a dark, dank wall of silent green forest. No one went near this small lake, although they began to log it the year I left the big lake.

I got such a strike that I thought my spoon must have fouled one of the sunken trees with which the bottom of that little lake fairly bristled. It was their projecting, skeleton tips which added so much to the melancholy of this lonely spot. When I seized the rod I knew that I had a fish, and, if I had any doubts, they were dispelled when the reel gave the exciting loud scream. It was a $12\frac{1}{2}$-lb. salmon. He broke once, then I did not see him again for half an hour, when I landed him. I know the time because I took a quick look at my wristwatch to see how long I had before night came down; it was a five-mile row home. And although the wind often dropped with the sun, it just as often freshened to a gale when darkness set in. What the salmon did was to 'sound,' bore straight to the bottom; then for the next half hour he kept trying to rub the hook out of him against every sunken stump on the bottom. It was a harrowing thirty minutes—for me. I don't know which of us was the weaker when I got him into the boat; my anxiety had taken such a lot of endurance out of me.

But when I saw him, his hooked jaws seemed to be defying me to eat him. Then I remembered the Germans, who were hungry, too. My way lay fairly close to them. And as the sun sank I came off their clearing. She, who had seen me coming down the lake, was standing on their float. At that time of the year I always took a shotgun along with me in case I might get a duck that was not too fishy—even the fine mallards eat the dead salmon, out in British Columbia!—and, if I had had good luck, I always shared it with these Germans. It gave me an excuse for shooting so many ducks! Her face fell when she saw the salmon, then it lighted:

'*Ach, so!* I shall boil him!'

I thought she meant to eat him then, but not that prudent housewife; she boiled that, and one or two other tolerably good salmon I gave her, and packed them in a salt-brine in jam jars against the coming winter.

When you have seen fish take on a value like that they acquire an additional meaning. Many a time by a stream in England, wondering how many I would bring home at the end of the day (to be displayed on a platter or on the floor of the local fishing hotel) I have thought of these fish in British Columbia, lying on the floor-boards of my boat, and what a feeling of deep satisfaction the sight of them always gave to me. For there lay a day well earned, for both sport and food.

Later, when the wind howled around that structure we lived in, and the snows of winter began to fall, even though they were light ones—warmed as we were by the Japan Current—I felt a slight chill of insecurity to see those rods put away. It was as if (and I have had the joke played on me) someone had stolen my crutches when I was trying to walk again. A prop was gone. There was more truth in this than the phrase indicates, for with a considerable amount of bone gone in my leg—a legacy from the last war—I could not go very deep into those forests for game. Tree fallen upon tree had made a gigantic floor of forest Jackstraws; I shot a pine grouse as I came out of my door one early morning, that towered and fell only fifty yards away in the woods. I was at least half an hour getting to where I thought it had fallen. Even my cat, the Moze, whom I was trying to train as a retriever, could not find it; though several times, in the spring, I had to take baby grouse away from her.

She of course missed the supply of fresh fish more than we. We raised her from a ball of grey fluff, so small that she trembled as she stood up to lap milk from my finger tip. She had a remarkable brain. We could almost get across to each other. Learning to run before she could walk, she knew what it meant when she saw me pulling my skiff up on shore: Fish!

She rubbed herself ingratiatingly against my legs, purring, as I cleaned whatever I brought home and waiting for the entrails and lovely heads. For a cat she had an epicure's life. Fish ducks were *foie gras* to her.

I have purposely used the word 'structure' in alluding to the remarkable place in which we lived. For it could be called neither bungalow nor cabin, yet it was made of peeled, unpainted logs. It was designed by a colonel in the Indian Army, a medical officer, who had spent over thirty years in India, the last twenty in Ladakh. He was a congenital hermit, seeking sanctuary in solitude, living chiefly on bean-powder soup, yet a man who, when well over sixty, could still pack an elk head and slim down the mountain trail on his head. He was well past that now; and when he let us use his cabin I was shocked to see three splendid Hardy rods stretched across ordinary coat hangers, their tips bending down like old carriage whips.

The unfortunate, but unforeseen, fault in the design of this house was that it was built against heat. It had one huge, central, lofty room; fine in India. But in British Columbia winters we sat with our faces being roasted by the heat of a log fire, while our behinds were practically taking on ice formations. Only one half of us was ever warm at one time. This made us hardy, and, ironically, increased our appetites, so that our bills from the Hudson's Bay Co. and the store down at the foot of the lake bit deep into our small capital during those three winter months. When the deer season was over, when the southward flights of duck had long since passed on, only an occasional blue-bill (shot more for an experiment than anything else) came free to our larder.

Wearing old buckskin gloves, smeared with duck-blood, I nailed ducks to trees in the woods behind our cabin, set two steel traps, and caught two raccoons. First, I am sorry to say, I caught two 'wildish' cats; they were, possibly, parents of the Moze; one certainly was the father of her quartette of kittens the next summer. It was a grim performance to stun them with a stick, seize the trap and push down on its spring, then chuck the cat away before it came round enough to bite or scratch me. I almost gave up the pursuit of the raccoon. Then one morning, sitting in the sun, I saw the 'domino' of a 'coon's mask markings staring at me. I didn't much like that, either. Still, trapping is trapping; and those two thick 'coon skins, with their lovely tails, made a collar which my wife wore even in London in years later on.

These two 'coon skins led to a scene with the English 'honorary' Game Warden. He did not like me. I do not blame him; he knew that I had shot a deer, *by moonlight*, the night before the season opened. He could not pin it on me, because when he was invited to eat some deer liver the next day—with that spicy tang of the salal berry—the season *had* opened. He could not prove at what precise hour of the clock that deer had fallen in the glade. (It was like tapestry, that night; the deer feeding in the silvered glade!) He was such a useful person himself, having made a fine life out here on nothing much more than strength of character, that he rather resented any stranger coming along, trying to repeat somewhat the same performance. He would have liked me better had I been more helpless. But I didn't happen to feel that way; I was uncouthly independent; and when the two raccoons were trapped I skinned them as skilfully I think as anyone around that neck of the woods could.

This is not bragging. For years, as a youngster, I had trapped muskrats for pin-money, getting a quarter each for the raw skin. I knew how to begin with one hind foot (now I was using an old safety razor blade) and then cut in a semi-circle up that leg, around the crotch, then down the other leg—then carefully *peel* the 'coon out. Cutting, actually prising, with a slightly duller knife, all the tissues as I went (too sharp a knife would have cut the skin), until, turned inside out, nothing but the empty skin lay in my hands. Making two 'spreaders' from cedar, such as you use drying the old-fashioned long white kid gloves, I then stretched the skin gently—coating it deeply with salt. The salt makes a good cure, stops the hair from dropping out afterwards (in Kenya we used pounds upon pounds of salt to proof the skin of a big lion I had shot); then, when the fat had begun to harden on the skin I spent the next several days carefully pulling it off—or rubbing it off with a stone. When the pelts were dry and stiff, with no smelly or rotting fat, I then asked the Game Warden where to send them to be cured at Victoria.

'But you must have a *license* to trap!' he gasped. Then, after curiously examining the cedar spreaders and the clean skins: 'Did *you* do these?'

Grudgingly, but generously—for he could have arrested me—he gave me the address of a tanner down at Vancouver. But: 'Do me a favour,' he said —'don't trap any more.' I told him I would not; and I didn't.

I was busy enough sawing and splitting firewood that first winter. It took at least one whole day every week. Then, articles were beginning to be bought in New York. The attempts at short stories were served back to me by return of post from the editors precisely as if I had been playing tennis with them. I was amassing a pile of rejection slips. But I was also acquiring the art (not that I've got it yet) of writing something like a short story; I was being ruined of course by trying to emulate Maupassant, O'Henry, Flaubert, and Somerset Maugham—all at the same time—and it is small wonder that my stiff bits of carpentry did not waken enthusiasm among hard-boiled editors. Then one of the great New York men, a 'star' in his day (but now incapacitated by a horrible accident) wrote: 'Look here, why the hell don't you write what *you* want to—what you see right before your eyes? Are you *blind?*' And about a month later the mail brought a bulky roll from the *New York Herald*, with my story covering the whole front page of its Magazine Section: The Saga of the Pacific Salmon.

Yes, things were moving. The trouble with me had been that I was searching for the exotic and passing by the everyday things that lay all around me—simply because I would not see their significance. In the logging camps, for instance, I—who had been raised on Ralph Connor, with his dramatic tales of log-jams, and battles between Canucks in the East Canada timber regions —went about trying to find dramatic gems; usually about fights.

'Fight?' exclaimed Swanson. 'Why? We ain't got time. Man's got to work when he's in the woods. An' a feller gets tired. Maybe, over on Railway Street in Vancouver, when they got a bit of booze in 'em, maybe some of these come-and-go loggers has a fight now and then. I yust can't remember no fight whatever, 'cept one feller here . . . he kicked an Englishman's face off with his caulks.'

Swanson turned up the sole of his lumberman's boot showing the caulks, the heavy spikes that let them 'run' the logs. 'How'd you like to get a faceful of them?'

He couldn't remember, however, what the fight had been about. So of course there was no story. He was a hopeless case. In two years, although we became so thick that he actually brought a deer he had shot out of season over to my place to skin and clean it, I got just one story from him—and that quite unknown to him. It was when he was interested in my cat's *accouchement*—'When is dat cat going to have dem damn kittens?'—and he said: 'I had a cat dat stopped a murder once.'

For that story I got $100—enough to keep the wolves away for months.

I am not digressing. The Saga of the Salmon had shown me where my heart lay. It had proved to me that my three useless arts—sailing, shooting, and fishing—were not useless things. With them I could make my life. Which, to a large extent, I have. But, above all else, that abusive letter from my damaged editor-friend in New York pointed out to me that I should *look*. I should acquire eyes that saw. That conveyed thoughts and questions to my brain which made me *reason*. Looked at this way, The Things in the Water took on an increasing interest from then on.

The mail was brought up to the store by a man-of-all-trades, who was also the local marten trapper (and a very intelligent trapper, too). Twice a week, on Wednesdays and Saturdays, from the railway thirty miles down below, his rickety old car's arrival at the store was the social event of the lake—most of us foregathered there. At first I used to row the five miles down twice weekly, then only on Saturdays; then I would let it slide a week. But always I trolled a spoon as I rowed, hoping to pick up a trout; and in the season I also took a shotgun along with me. There was a patch of spruce on the low shore below me, with some flakes of open water behind them, in which the mallards used to lie, coming out high (as they do) beating their wings over the tree tops . . . before they turned, circling, down the sky. They offered some beautiful shots.

Then an occasional widgeon came belting past, a bald-pate; and these widgeon, who never seemed to eat the dead salmon, were a prize. Butter-balls, blue-bills, and golden-eye were with us most of the time. Down at the store, waiting for the mail (and we nearly always had to wait), I would try a Devon or troll the spoon around the river pool. Time was well filled in that place to which people wrote me from home, inquiring: 'What *can* you find to do with yourself?'

My wife, who became even more *farouche* than I about not seeing people, seldom came down to the store. But on one of these trips she caught the best Rainbow we got in British Columbia. It was a brutal day in the rainy season (and it rains for two months steady), when we were both wrapped in oil-skin slickers. On our way down I had got three golden-eye ducks, which now lay in the bow of our boat, with my wife huddled in the stern, holding our can-vas mail-and-supply bag under her slicker to keep things dry, the rod cocked through her arm. We had almost forgotten the line trolling astern, when, coming into our bay, the reel suddenly began to scream. It was too fast to make us think that we had fouled something in the lake. And too fast to be peremptorily halted. I told my wife to put as much drag on with her thumb as she could, without risking a broken line; and the answer was a beautiful Rainbow trout coming clear out of the water several hundred feet astern.

By that time you could almost see the spindle of the spool. Nearly all the line had been taken out. This meant that the Rainbow already had a lot of 'backing,' which was an old line that I didn't trust. If he had made another run he would unquestionably have got away, but he took it into his head to go down. Pushing the skiff towards him as fast as I could, we won back all the backing and were now on the good line. He had taken a little Pflueger trout-spoon, with a row of scarlet beads between the two spoons, and a single hook. My wife's braking had been strong enough to drive the hook into him, even if his first drive at it had not done that. It was now merely a question of not doing something silly.

He was a beautiful fish, in fine fighting shape. She was standing upright in the pouring rain, our letters, new books, and bread absorbing it all like blotters, more determined than even I could be to see that *this* big one did not get away. She was terrified. The fish was telegraphing shocks to her with each of his struggles down in the water. Between us and the bay proper was a semi-submerged island with a very shallow patch between it and the mainland where the bottom moss almost grew to the surface. The Rainbow made for that. 'Now we've lost him!' gasped my wife despairingly, for he jumped, bringing a line full of moss out of the water. It was as if you had thrown a wave-crest of seaweed into the air. But it was with this that he probably killed himself, for when I pushed the skiff onto him as fast as I could, we saw him swimming ahead of us pushing a headload of this long tapering green plant. We did not dare get too near, in case he made a quick run under the boat, or jumped again with that short line. I saw the pinkish stripe along his side, and his big tail working feebly. I told her to pull him gently around. Then I slipped the net under his head and flapped him in the boat—before he fell out of it. He weighed $6\frac{3}{4}$ lb.

Now, as I have stressed before, mere size does not count; I know you may catch 25-lb. Rainbow in New Zealand, but this wasn't New Zealand; and this one, late in the season though he was, was a perfect fish. Had we been in England I should probably have had him mounted. We thought him so good to look at that it seemed a shame to eat him. But we grilled some of him that night and boiled the rest, which we put outside in our wire larder, having a good glut of cold Rainbow trout for both lunch and dinner the next day, not forgetting a large hunk rowed across to the Germans. This was caught on the old Bristol bait rod that I had bought in 1911 and used so much for bass. And on this rod I caught three salmon in the river-pool while I was waiting for the mail: 12½, 8½, 7½ lb. The smallest we ate ourselves, the two others going to the Germans, who boiled them and pickled them in jam jars. The big one broke my line some forty feet from the spoon, raced into the flooded under-brush (it was full rainy season then); and I caught him again because the line fouled in the brush and held him till I rowed over to him. But by that time it took really a strong stomach to eat these salmon so far gone towards spawning. So I gave it up, except for spearing some fresh-run salmon down by the tidal mouth of the river with the Siwash Indians.

When the salmon are running you can find a Siwash village in the night—blindfold. The stench is unbelievable. The reason is that their villages of unpainted board shacks, with the grotesque, carved totem poles standing outside them, are nearly always established near a shallow reach of river in which the salmon can be speared. The men stand there, throwing spears into salmon, throw the ten- or fifteen-pound fish to their squaws; the squaws slit them open, jerk out their insides, and throw these over their shoulders up the bank. The overpowering effect of some thousands of salmon interiors putrefying in the hot sun leaves you searching for words. It is appalling.

These particular Siwash were using a spear with two steel barbs on a Y-shaped tip. The barbs each had a little lanyard holding them to the main shaft. And the shaft had a lanyard which the thrower attached to his little finger. They threw the spear in the way the ancient Greeks threw the javelin —*not* held in the middle, but propelled from fingers placed against the butt. They thus threw it into the air in a parabola—letting it *fall* into a fish, not throwing it into him.

This distinction must be grasped in order to appreciate their skill. Because they not only had to allow for refraction—which makes you think the salmon is further away from you than he actually is—but also for the speed of the fish, allowing the spear to drop as the salmon was passing under it. Yet they hardly ever missed.

I, seizing the spear by the middle—and throwing well under where the water-refraction made him appear to be—drove both barbs deep into my first salmon—and merely aroused smiles. A patient Siwash, when I drew the fish in, politely showed me how my clumsy, strong-arm method had merely succeeded in ruining a salmon for smoking. Not only had I broken its back; I had mucked the fish about with the spear driven half through him.

It was a tremendous sight. It ended with one of those sunsets when all the world is dusted with a golden powder, and the salmon passing up the river, slow-flowing down here at the sea-coast, passing, passing, passing . . . like the very legends the Siwash had built around them. You could understand mythology, and animal worship, when you stood on that raw river bank, with these Japanese-faced Indians (the Haida unquestionably have come across from Asia), and realised that for thousands of years these Indians had almost certainly been spearing salmon on the same spot on which you stood. The world was now fast-changing around them, but two elements remained constant in the scene—the Indian and the salmon. Their relationship to each other remained the same. Before steel, the barbs were made of bone or, possibly, walrus ivory. That was the only essential difference.

We witnessed the last potlach in the House-So-Big-That-One-Has-To-Shout-To-Be-Heard—which is a literal translation of the Siwash name for the vast barn-like structure of cedar planks in which these coastal Indians used to revel in their passion for dancing. It had no chimney. The fire in its centre was made of huge lengths of tree trunks—and a tower of red sparks roared, like a continual blast, up through a large hole in the pointed roof high above. Inside were seats where the tribes sat, ranged in tiers. They beat on these seats with wooden sticks, chanted, and men danced with wooden masks around the fire. Some of these masks were significantly like the Japanese 'horror' masks. Their scale was strange to the occidental ear—at times like the Chinese. *Then suddenly you felt it in your pulse beats.* You found yourself swaying, vibrating, to a thing you did not understand. They danced, with these masks, the Dance of the Bear, the Wolf, and the Tyee—the big King Salmon, which goes up to 100 lb.

They went into frenzies, threw themselves on the sand, with mouths flecked with foam. This, too, they had done for thousands of years. You were taken back until something unknown moved inside your own soul; you were plagued by the feeling that stirred uneasily in your own flesh and bones. Had you, on the long road to the You of today, ever danced like that?

This is not fantasy. As I watched the 'Doctor' dance of the Bushmen on the edge of the Kalahari Desert in upper South-West Africa (nineteen years later), an unheard note in their cries swept me back instantly to that starry

46

night by the river in British Columbia. There is no ethnological connection between Bushman and Siwash—except at the very beginning of the origin of man—yet there was the same totem worship in both these primitive dances. In the Kalahari, after the Doctor dance in which four Bushmen witch doctors danced an initiate into a complete state of hypnosis, the tiny men danced the Dance of the Kudu around the thorn fire—putting their fingers up on either side of their little chimpanzee heads to imitate its horns. And the high chanting of the tiny Bushwomen was weirdly similar to that of the Siwash squaws.

I trolled across the salt inlet of that river in British Columbia when the leaping salmon were so thick that the white bursts of water from their breaking and falling back made me think the bay was covered with 'white horses.' This is far from being any exaggeration, as anyone knows who has seen the salt mouths of British Columbia rivers when the big run was on. Neither is it a fish story, for, although I thought dozens of times that a salmon was going to fall on his next leap into my boat—I never caught one.

The ex-Royal Air Force major with me, however, caught a 10-lb. fish with a spoon he had painted bright scarlet. 'It's the red that gets 'em!' he exulted. Red seems a colour which induces fish to strike all over the world—the bass of the United States; the salmon of British Columbia; the trout of the Shetlands, striking at a Peter Ross.

And so we went up to the lonely lake again, into the dead of winter, where rods, rifle and shotgun were put away until spring.

III

Saga of the Pacific Salmon

For over a month in the autumn it rains steadily on Vancouver Island, while the fogs curl through the forests and the mists from the Pacific are swept in. This northland has a melancholy grandeur then. And it is then that you may witness the end of the salmon's fore-doomed life span. You see the final act of the tragedy. You may witness, if you have the luck to realise its drama, the beginning of the new life.

Down below the river pool lived a Scot who had pitted himself against inexorable Nature to 'better the odds,' as he phrased it, of the Pacific salmon's chance for life. He was the hatchery-man. But he was so much more than that, such a fanatic, such a high priest of his cult that wherever since I have been fishing the picture always comes back to me of him standing there on that fish trap in British Columbia, performing his almost mystic rites.

Great green and purple rocked mountains; storm clouds pouring in from the Pacific; driving rain drenching the forests; forests of spruce, of cedar, of fir—thick as the hair on the back of a dog—a wind-twisted, crashing maelstrom. We could hear the thundering roar of the Robinson, sluicing down to the sea, its rapids milk-white, foaming, swift as a hydraulic jet. A wild day, even for British Columbia when the rains are on. We could hardly row against the swift river.

'Hell,' said the hatchery man; 'I don't think we'll make it!'

I couldn't talk. 'Just one more stroke and then die!' I groaned to myself (I said the same thing for two miles at the Poughkeepsie boat races); and at last we entered the reach.

'McPherson,' I said, when the spots had cleared from my eyes, 'the salmon aren't worth it. Nothing is worth so much torture.'

McPherson was lighting his pipe—upside down—defiant of rain. He bobbed his head at the pool. I looked over the side. And saw the Red Host.

Great, red, pale-eyed salmon stared up from its depths; an army passed, phantom-like, underneath. Weary, covered with sores, they shot in from

48

their fight with the stream, rested, and then silently took up their pilgrimage again. Thousands and thousands of salmon, up from the sea, to spawn and then die.

'Ghosts?'

'Aye,' said McPherson, 'they're ghosts, right enough. Come three weeks every one will be dead. Look at that buck! He's half-dead already.'

I looked at the fish: diseased, distorted, miserable thing. It seemed hard to believe that only a month or so back he had flashed through the salt water like silver. Then had come the Urge; he had turned his nose towards fresh water—the stream he had been born in two years before. The scales had dropped off his back, to be replaced by soft spongy flesh; his jaws had become hooked, the teeth emerging, until like some savage red dog he entered the Straits of Juan de Fuca. Fasting, intent on his mission, he had escaped the weirs, wheels, and nets of the canners, fought the swollen flood of the river, leaped, twisted and mounted the falls, won past the spears of the Siwash—

'I have seen them,' McPherson broke in on my thoughts, 'a male and a female, comin' up stream, with a gang of Rainbows trailing their wake, like a wolf-pack hanging on to the flank. Aye, and I've seen the old buck turn and chase them away from her.'

'Guts!' McPherson grated the words. 'Pound for pound, inch for inch, the salmon's the gamest thing in the world. And you say they're not worth it!'

Salmon, to me, had once been something that came in a tin. A hint to the grocer would land the thing on my table. But McPherson was telling me things.

'An' for what? In a few weeks every one will be dead. They'll raise a stink in the land. You'll see them clogging the bars; this water will fall and leave them in lines on the banks. Ducks will come in here in swarms and stuff themselves so full of dead, rotten fish that their own flesh will taste worse than poison. The mallards stuff themselves; they'll feed on nothing but eyes. Aye, and the bears make a bloody mess on the snows. Millions and millions of salmon get snuffed out like a candle.'

'Why?' I asked meekly.

McPherson gave a snort: 'Why! Now ask me another. Could I, or any other man, tell you why Nature is the damn fool that she is? You and I wouldn't be sitting out here in this tub in this damned awful weather.'

(All five species of the *Oncorhynchus*—the Pacific salmon—spawn but once and then die. Sockeye, Spring, and Dog Salmon have a four years' cycle of life; Cohoes and Humpbacks two years. In some cases, such as the Fraser River and the Naas, there is also a small run of Sockeyes, having a five-year life-cycle.)

Coming up-lake in the hatchery launch, a condemned Japanese fisherman, McPherson had talked of his work, explaining the need for such effort. Between Nature and Man, he contended, the salmon is on the verge of extinction. Left an orphan at birth (could you call an egg that?) a salmon egg has just one chance in a thousand of producing a fish that will eventually return to complete the tragic life-cycle of his existence, i.e., to propagate his species. One in a thousand! A bad chance, indeed. Hence the hatchery.

The hatchery betters the odds, gets the fish out of the egg, past the yolk-sac, the fry, and well into the fingerling stage . . . and then turns him loose. He is a bit of a lad then, able to take care of himself; and even a cutthroat trout will have to move, and think, fast to catch him. Thus spoke McPherson:

'Eggs! Give me the eggs, and enough retaining ponds—and I'll re-stock the ocean.'

There are people who maintain that the hatcheries have not proved their worth, that all their work is but a drop in the bucket; but this hatchery man was so convinced by the evidence of his own eyes that he did not even answer my hints along this line. He stood there on the rim of the fish-trap, with a salmon clasped by the tail. His right elbow pinioned its head to his side. McPherson's trained hand slid along the Cohoe's stomach towards the vent. A stream of cornelian globules shot into the galvanised iron bucket, beautiful things, about the size of a currant. 'She's a bonny fush,' said McPherson. He spoke as if he were milking a prize Holstein.

'A marvellous fish. Let's have another.'

I dipped the net into the box formed by the upright wooden slats of the trap, and chased a fish around until I caught it. 'Buck,' said McPherson, after the barest glance. The mittened left hand closed over the tail; the fifteen-pound fish swung and a quick flip of that well-trained elbow imprisoned the head. Again the nubbly, intelligent fingers slid towards the vent. A stream, fluid this time, quite milk-like shot into the pail. He turned and directed it into another pail, full of those amber-red eggs. Then he flung the fish back into the swirling, discoloured stream, where, as far as I can make out, it swam off feeling quite cheery and bright.

Millions and millions of salmon get snuffed out like a candle

Like a research worker in his laboratory, the Scot peered into the bucket, and gently let a soft flow of water seep in over the brim and across the fertilising eggs.

'Watch it now!' said McPherson.

I watched a miracle take place in the pail. A mist floated over the eggs, almost imperceptible, so fine was its fabric. It was the 'changing of colour.' Now each egg was distinct, wrapped in its own little robe of Creation. A white spot on each showed that Life was now there.

Some quickly turned a light coral in colour. These McPherson deftly extracted and cast from him. They were already dead. He went over his 'babies.'

By now I was feeling his fatherly interest. I went after the last fish in the trap. A queer pair, the two of us, the Scot and I in that mountain stream in British Columbia; and a queer fish, that in the trap. A thumping big buck, already far gone towards spawning; the hook nose and dog-teeth showing plainly. Some male salmon are so distorted this way, with the growth of reproductive organs inside them, that the jaws shut on each side of each other like shears. This fellow looked vicious. Also, the fish trap was but a rickety contraption. We faced each other. The pale, yellow-eyed salmon seemed to be eyeing me malevolently.

'Whush! man'—the landing net was snatched from my hand, and with one deft, practised dab McPherson ended the battle. In a trice the big fish was locked in his grip. McPherson leant over the pail again.

I like to remember him there, mist-wreaths curling about him, smoke-like, his red beard aflame. He might have been some High Priest conducting a rite, a Siwash *shaman*, perhaps, for the myths of the Haida Indians are peopled with salmon. The Haida had a belief that if a woman ate salmon eggs she would be turned into stone. High-prowed canoes, Siwash, McPherson, the salmon; they all belonged to this picture. The old Northwest that is passing. And McPherson, with his pails of red eggs, was fighting a rearguard action. Against . . . ? Well, against Time, perhaps; Time and the Canners.

'A godless lot!' said McPherson of the canners, 'with thought for naught but themselves.'

Their money has made them a power in British Columbia politics. Strong enough to defeat (up to that time) any laws being made that would place a ban upon unlimited fishing. 'Money,' cursed McPherson, ''tis all they are after. Catch all the fish they can—*and to hell with posterity!*'

And the Future was the particular concern of McPherson. 'Take care of those eggs!' He eyed me appraisingly before handing over the buckets. I stood there in the stream, the water pouring into my boots: 'Take care of the eggs!' I retorted. 'If you're not quick about passing them to me I'll pitch the whole lot in the drink.' For an instant a fierce light blazed in the blue eyes above me. Panther hunters have seen it when in chase of the cub. I waded hurriedly off into the stream, the sacred buckets held high overhead.

McPherson, with magnificent assurance, ran along the 3″ × 3″ wall of the fish trap, and so got to shore. We made our way through dank undergrowth, dripping alders, devil's-club thorns, around the pillar-like trunks of gigantic spruce; and at last deposited the black-painted buckets safely on the floor-boards of our rowboat. But the danger was not yet behind us; there was the river.

Great snags hurtled past us; gaunt, twisted branches, clawing arm-like at the air. A merganser came like a bullet up stream, making time—his red, wicked head stretched out like a spear-point. 'Yon bloody bird!' blasphemed McPherson. 'Every time he sticks his head under water—he comes up with a fish in his mouth.'

We watched the saw-bill shoot out of sight around a bend. 'Here's hoping we don't hit one of those snags,' said McPherson. It was like shooting-the-chutes at the White City. How a fish ever got up that current was a puzzle to me. We had only been able to get up the river by abandoning oars and pulling ourselves up by seizing the branches of the flooded banks. McPherson declared that a salmon could round a rock in a current running six hundred feet to the minute. It takes a seven-mile current, running steadily, to bar their continuous progress. 'And they use their heads!' said McPherson. 'They make use of every obstruction, sneak up in the backwaters and eddies—and then charge the swift water. Like *that!*' McPherson's fist shot past my nose to show the speed of their dash. It stunned you, the thought of this Homeric struggle, with Death as its final reward.

This yearly pilgrimage of the salmon made you wonder if, after all, there had not been some mistake made in the order of things. Fish like the *Tyee*, the Spring Salmon, which very often reaches a size of 100 lb., blotted out in their prime. It was too much like killing a man when he's forty.

We were now on the grey, sea-going launch and headed down the lake, where McPherson was going to drop me at my place. For the first time that day he relaxed. We had 'stripped' thirteen fish. Three bucks and ten hen salmon. At 2,000 eggs to the Cohoe female, that meant that we had collected 20,000 potential salmon. Twenty fish would, by the estimated average, be all that Nature would have allowed to mature—twenty fish! But these eggs were now the protégés of McPherson.

They would be placed in long, wire, water-flowing troughs at the hatchery. In about 90 days queer little things would emerge. Fish about the size of a pin, with an odd little sac fastened to each. (The yolk-sac; its meals for four weeks.) When the sac would disappear the fish would be placed in retaining ponds and fed with grated ox-liver. They would live high on this and wax fat and strong. (I saw hatchery men, years afterwards, feeding ox-liver to the trout in a Somerset hatchery.) In about four months they would be about the size of one's finger—fingerlings. 'But, this year,' contended McPherson, 'I'm going to keep them beyond that—say, six months or so. As long as I can. That will increase their chances. Every day adds. Then I can put them into the stream and not say, "God be with you," and think it's a joke.'

But McPherson was, nevertheless, depressed. He claimed that the miscalculations of an engineer, over on the mainland, had, some years back, practically ruined the world's best run of salmon. And no man could put it back.

A few figures—'on the wrong side of the decimal point!' said McPherson —and a cliff face blew off that was not intended to blow off; it fell into the Fraser River, just when the 'big run' was on; it blocked the river; and— '*Bang!* went the world's best supply of tinned fish.'

'What would you say,' he asked, eyeing me for any dramatic reactions, 'if I told ye that one push of a man's hand—the hand that touched off that dynamite blast—cost the Province of British Columbia, *and* the State of Washington, U.S.A., twenty-seven million dollars?'

'I would say you were balmy.'

But McPherson, despite the gorgeous chance for histrionics in the grim tale he had to tell, was precise with his figures. Years afterwards, all over the world—being offered 'Pink' salmon, instead of the Red Sockeye—I felt the brunt of this mathematician's blunder. Genuine Red salmon had become hard to get—even the price of the 'Pink' had gone up; all of which you may find out easily for yourself when you try to buy salmon at any store.

The reason for this world-catastrophe is another freak of Nature, in her seemingly reckless treatment of the salmon, known as the 'Big Run' on the Fraser River. For some reason that has never yet been discovered there was a run of Sockeye salmon up the Fraser *every fourth year* that was always far bigger than the combined runs of the previous three years put together. This run occurred at precise intervals: 1909, 1913, etc., and would have continued —had it not been for this accident—again in 1917, 1921, 1925, and so on. This run was so big that even the most heartless fishing of the cannery companies, the traps and spearing of the Indians, the puny kills by sportsmen—nothing could even deplete it. Fish, massing into the Fraser on those Big Years, actually used to fight for space on the spawning beds. Nearly all the Sockeye in the world (the former commercial salmon) were hatched out on those beds. It is said that the three lean years—which even then were rich with salmon— could not aggregate to half the over-crowded 'big year.'

But when they were building the Canadian Northern Railway's tunnel at Yale in 1913, an engineer underestimated the strength of a blast he had ordered. Instead of breaking loose merely a calculated cubic quantity of rock, it knocked the entire face of the cliff into the river.

'It was a sight to make a man scream,' said McPherson (who had been called over to help). 'I watched thousands and thousands of salmon have a try at that leap. Men worked like beavers to help the fish past. We built fish-ladders on the side flumes; we hauled away boulders by sheer sweat alone. I tore the nails off me hands. We were frenzied, you know—we knew what it meant, if that Big Run did not get past. But it was no use. Millions and millions of fish died at the foot of the water shooting over those fallen rocks. They couldn't make it. Nine feet—the fish made the height—but they couldn't face a fire-hose. That's what it was like. Your heart broke when you saw that water hit them and hurl them back. With their eggs still inside them, they died—and with them died the Big Run of the Fraser.'

McPherson declared that it was the most gigantic catastrophe known in the history of fishes. 1917—which should have been another 'Big Year'— showed an 81 per cent decrease of catch. It was certain that the Big Run could never be brought back. And for some years after the 1913 disaster the Canadian Government and the State of Washington could not agree upon a closed period for the Fraser. Too much money had been invested in the rival canning industries. Canners claimed that they could not stop—they must fish every year to cover their overheads. Interest must be paid, posterity notwithstanding, upon Capital. And, as the first twenty-five miles of the Fraser happens to run through American territory, there seemed no answer. Tit-bits of reform, eyewash for the Public, were achieved in making some of the poor Siwash Indians sell out their fishing rights.

In 1921—another 'Big Year'—the catch was 93 per cent less than that of 1913.

The Hon. William Sloane, Commissioner of Fisheries in British Columbia, declared: 'Unless some radical steps are taken at once the salmon will soon be as extinct as the Dodo.'

Years later (I do not know the exact date) an agreement of a sort was reached for a closed period to protect the runs on the Fraser. I do not know its result. It has not, from what I can see, yet made any effect on the market, and I write this as a purely personal affair—yours and mine. When your grocer offers you a tin of salmon with 'PINK' on the label—whitish, queer-looking stuff, not at all like the firm, reddish flesh we were once so accustomed to seeing against the green salad and mayonnaise, you may think of this death of the 'Big Year' on the Fraser.

For this pinkish stuff is not Sockeye. It is usually Dog Salmon, a fish that until the 'Big Run' was destroyed and rejected by the canners—despised. Only fit for a Siwash! Humpbacks are now sold as 'Pinks.' By law, these names must be put on the labels. That is one bit of ethics which the Government have observed. The reason for the lack of colour in these fish is that the nature of their life-cycle is such that they are already advanced with their spawning process before they reach fresh or tidal waters where they can be caught by the canners; reproduction has concentrated the colour-giving oil from their bodies into their eggs or milt.

They aren't bad. But I'd rather have catfish and waffles.

Ducks at sunset. The mallards usually stayed up on the lake. And they were putrid from eating dead salmon. But every sunset there was a flight up of the ducks which had been feeding down in the salt water all day. On calm evenings they came over high, winging their bullet-like way to sanctuaries far up the long lake. Against a head wind they came low, and they frequently took advantage of any lee of land. Sitting in my skiff behind the underbrush of a long point, with a box of cartridges spilled into my felt hat on the floor boards, I could get some fine shots. After darkness set in I often heard their *wissh!* of wings come close to my head as they dropped into our own bay. Naturalists may contest the point, insisting that parent birds teach their young nothing; that both flight and nest-building are an *inherited* knowledge, not the product of instruction, but I *know* that ducks teach their young to fly and land. Next spring I used to watch a pair of mallards circle our bay again and again with their young ones, incontestably giving them both flying and landing lessons. I watched, rowing after her, a hooded merganser duck, with her flotilla of young ducklings, far out from shore, as she shot back and forth behind them on the water (they were too young to fly), driving them like any well-trained sheep dog to the camouflaging safety of the bushes along the shore. With their fluffy black-and-yellow markings they were almost invisible! I would be within a yard or so of a little one, looking straight at it but not seeing it, until I noticed its little black-button eye. Meanwhile the mother was flying up and down the lake behind me, trying to distract my attention.

They say the teal drake migrates ahead of the duck, or *vice versa*. I don't know. I usually found them together; but I never knew *where* I would find them. I would not have been surprised to see one get out of my bed. These little teal were never fishy. Neither were they plentiful. I have stumbled on them in a patch of water left by the rains when, at dusk, I have pulled up my skiff at a lonely, low clearing, hoping to put up a pheasant. The golden-eye used to lie in the little off-lake I have been talking about. Sitting in my skiff at the mouth of the channel which connected it with the big lake, I would fire one shot, and quickly re-load, to bring them out. Ducks, when they can, always fly over water.

So they would come, almost too high by the time they came over. The English aristocrat who lived on that side loved this shooting, for he could hit duck I often thought were out of range. He was a remarkable shot. But, like most people who live long out there, he had given up fishing and shooting after a time. Sitting in that channel mouth one stormy winter sunset, with a heavy sea running on the lake outside, I saw a black shape coming at me from the grey lake that I thought must be a loon. Something when it cocked its wings to light made me suspect it wasn't. So I shot.

My shotgun was only a 16 bore; I had in nothing but 5's, a general load I used for nearly everything; and my first shot, as this mysterious bird was coming at me head on, seemed like the proverbial water on a duck's back. The big bird went over me like a heavy bomber. Then I swung round and gave it the choke in its trousers. When it hit the water and turned over I found I had shot a fine Canada goose.

You can imagine the excitement in my cabin that night! We ate nearly the whole bird at one sitting. But that was the only goose I shot, or even saw, in those two years. They usually skipped the lake on their long south-ward flight. What this particular bird's story was I could never know—except the end of it.

One day, in British Columbia, you will wake up and find that the snow-flaked mountain opposite you has lost its flat, metallic colours of white, blue, and rock-grey. And the lake itself, instead of looking black as ink against the white snow marge, is a bowl of quivering blue haze. The sun feels unusually hot on your face. You can *smell* the forest behind you. Spring has come.

This was the real fishing! Spring, with the fly. I used practically the same flies I would use in Scotland, with the addition of the Cowichan Coachman, which has a plum and white wing, invented and tied by an English lady down on the coast. The seductive Alexander I found a dud in British Columbia, though I heard of other people having spectacular luck with it. Butcher, Zulu, the old reliable March Brown, Silver Doctor, Jock Scott, Grouse and Claret, Teal and Green, Teal and Red, with the exception of the Peter Ross (which I did not have there), these were the same flies you would use in Scotland, the Shetlands, or the Outer Isles. I nearly always used the Butcher for a tail fly, the Zulu for a dropper, and rang the changes with the inter-mediate fly. I used the same set-up in the Balkans, in the swift mountain streams of the Dinaric Alps with equal (if not better) success—plus the Peter Ross and particularly the hackle Blue Upright. I took the side-gangs off my spinning baits, finding I caught more fish by trusting solely to the tail gang. They didn't foul-hook so much, or near-hook. And I found a 2-inch, gold and silver, flat 'Reflex' Devon—with one scarlet bead at its tail above the treble hook—outstandingly the best artificial lure. Again I emphasise the deadly attraction of that red or scarlet.

I had secured my house-boat then, this unpainted board shack built on a long raft of cedar logs; and in the lonely neck below Bald Mountain, where I moored it the next spring, I could always see the trout swimming about us in the calm of the early morning. I'll confess that in the very early spring I caught them with night-lines, baited with the illegal salmon eggs; but that was before they would take the fly. One had to live! I have caught them from our raft; but usually I left them alone in my vicinity. There was one big buck trout who *lived* under our raft. We used to watch him coming out—he used

I had secured my house-boat then

it for shade on the very hot days—and we could see him investigating the various bits of food we threw over to tempt him. We often debated whether he knew he was safe or not.

The partner of the Englishman who lived across the lake had come from tea-planting in Ceylon, found that the 'ranch' in British Columbia was not the paradise he had expected when he sank his money in it, and he was soured. About the only thing that interested him now was fishing. He rowed across to me one dawn with the remark that he heard the Rainbow had started to take the fly 'like anything!' in the river down below. What about it?

I don't know which is the most exciting: the thud when a fish takes the wet fly under the water, the 'sup' as some big fish will turn and take a dry fly down—just before you hit him—or the last moments when you are, anxiously, about to land him. All of them of course surpass anything that a spinning bait can give you. There is nothing like the fly, or the pleasure of casting it.

On this swift river a line of logs had been laid along the other bank, linked by short sections of chain, to shunt off down-coming drift wood, brush, logs or whatever came down from the lake, so as to keep the river open. These early trout seemed to be lying always along those logs. It was not an easy cast owing to the high brush behind you, but when it fell and you saw your line sweeping down you knew that at any second the strike might come. A two-pounder would be a good fish in that swift water—too much if he took to the white water right away. Our bags were never very large, perhaps ten each in a day. A 2½-pound fish was the biggest I remember getting there. But with a fresh spring wind blowing around you and that joy of being just alive, which comes after the long winter, every day was exhilarating.

There was a pool below where the house-boaters, and those who lived near the store, had a miraculous rise on some evenings. I have fished it with three or four boats on it, with fish rising all around us.

The back-drop of all this was the heavy fir forest, with the mountains above the timber line shining in the sun high above. The Cutthroat ran larger, but did not seem to have the same drive that animated the fine fighting Rainbow. Nor were they so good to eat. And by far the most memorable fish to me from those two years were two 2½-lb. Rainbow, alike to the ounce, that I caught within half an hour of each other in my own bay. Both of them put up such a battle that I thought they must be four pounds at least. We were so sure of a fish when we wanted one that one night when we had invited the old Irish doctor over to dinner I didn't go out until the very last minute. The consequence was that I did not get a rise. Darkness had come down. I saw the long oblong of light from the open door of our house-boat, even heard the doctor's voice, sarcastically inquiring had I gone down to *buy* a fish from the hatchery—when a big brute, about three pounds, took my fly while it was sinking to the bottom.

Several times in the darkness he got under my boat without my knowing it, until I heard his fins and tail fluttering as he jumped behind me on the other side. My wife and the doctor, too, could hear the splashes; and he called—'Is that our dinner?' I called back that I thought it was. Then, with the fish in the boat, I yelled back triumphantly: 'All right, Eve—put on the frying-pan.'

Fish were no treat to the doctor; he was tired of them. But even his weary palate woke up when he had that one in crisp fillets, with *sauce mayonnaise*. Though he said grudgingly: 'Seems an unholy waste of good mayonnaise.' The fact was that the people who lived in those parts simply did not like fish. And as for salmon, they preferred it from a tin. I felt slightly that way about the British Columbia salmon myself, for it has nothing like the taste of a Scotch fish—no, it doesn't come within at least three thousand miles of it!— which is the distance across Canada.

But that spring I had so much work to do that an hour or so's fishing at sunset was an anticipated relaxation. I was working hard a good part of each day staining wood, making furniture, getting our house-boat in order. Then when the lake began slowly to fall as the melting snows vanished I marooned big logs on shore by wedging rocks under them, which logs, when the water fell, I thereupon began to cut up for our summer and winter firewood. The old German helped with a long two-handed saw to cut the sections, and I helped him; then we each split up our own kindling wood. The sawing was a back-breaking job, for that German was a very tough and stubborn man, whose pride would not let him suggest taking a minute's breathing spell unless he was dead sure that I was ready for it. My flannel shirt dripped with sweat. Then, after a quick, naked dip into the lake, some fresh dry slacks and a clean shirt . . . the hour or so that I would idly fish along the shore was a luxury. These fish cleaned and lazily eaten, I would sit out in a camp chair on our 'deck' and watch the stars come out. It is not an easy philosophy to trap with mere words—the feeling is not even tangible to yourself—but there was a peculiar 'justification' in nights such as this which only 'settlers' can feel. They will know, who read these pages. Then I would go to bed and contentedly read myself to sleep by the soft light of the old-fashioned oil lamp between our two cots. I read more good books out in British Columbia, and got more out of them, than I have anywhere since. In the morning, very often with the dawn, I would wake up with mind and muscles rested, take a dip overside after I had got the fire going and put on the coffee; or, if my wife was still sleeping soundly (which she seemed able to do until broad daylight), I would try a few casts before breakfast. Frankly, I preferred a good dish of bacon and eggs, with a slab of fried bread, to fish for breakfast; and we ordered our eggs from the Hudson's Bay Co. by the gross.

It was a delectable life. There were no mosquitoes to contend with, no pests, no neighbours (unless we wanted them), we owed no one in the world any money; I cannot imagine why we ever left it. I now put in several hours every day in hard writing, and had reached that point in the short-story technique where I was fairly certain that when I finished a story I would sell it. If I ever managed to finish it—which was quite another thing. But this certainty of having my stuff bought was the switch-over from the amateur to the professional attitude toward my work. It gave me satisfaction, security, and almost a ravenous interest in the use of words. The day when I realised I was checking and guiding the emotional impulse by a conscious control of form and words—was the day I ceased being frightened of having 'no visible means of support.'

From then on British Columbia could have been a paradise for us. We knew we could have lived there until we died. We had already been in communication with Alaska to get a small boat, with a sail, in which we intended that summer to cruise around Glacier Bay, but when that next looked-for spring came along, and we had already got so far as selecting the kit which we would take with us up to Alaska, I suddenly saw that if we did that trip we would be in British Columbia forever. And there was a lot of the world I still wanted to see.

So we talked this over. My wife wept. She, of all the people I have ever known, was eminently suited for this life in British Columbia. She was self-sufficient both physically and mentally. She loved this lake, she loved the woods, she loved the absolute freedom of our existence. But she, too, thought that we should not 'quit,' retire in British Columbia, just yet. So she reluctantly agreed.

It was a sad night, that night—with the first of the up-coming salmon splashing as they jumped in the moonlight by our house-boat. The next morning I went down to have one last try for a big steelhead. They were running now, the river packed with 10-lb. fish. But although I fished over them all day, trying every fly in the book, not one of them would look at it.

'Don't that beat the very devil!' shouted a man across the river, who declared he had come all the way up from Seattle just to fish this spring steelhead run. 'I'm a-going to just take my damn rod apart and go home!'

I told him I was going to do the same thing. The next week we were on a train crossing the Rockies, bound for Chicago. I was going back to make money, all the money I could. This time it was going to be for a bigger jump. It was. Two years later I threw up the best-paying and most promising job I will ever have, sailed for England, bought a 26-foot Norfolk Broads yawl and sailed from the North to the Black Sea. But—

If I had caught one big steelhead that spring morning in British Columbia, both of us would be there now.

IV

The spell of the Shetlands; on the northwest tip of Scotland; and gillies

Fishing, as I have said, is a combination of many things, fish themselves not always being the main object. Therefore it will not seem perverse for me to say that I have enjoyed fishing in the north of Scotland, the Shetlands, and the Hebrides, even more than I did out in British Columbia. That is the truth. For sheer grandeur I doubt if there is anywhere a more magnificent part of the world than you will find in the Shetlands. Sea trout caught in the salt estuaries or in those peaty burns, or brown trout taken among the granite ledges of the windy lochs, will provide you with memories with which you can invigorate yourself for the rest of your life.

The Shetlands are a paradox. The very islands themselves do not look like islands but seem an ice-rubbed, battered mountain range that has suddenly sunk below its timber line into the sea. There are over a hundred islands. The biggest, Mainland, which takes up over three-fourths of all the surface, is fifty-four miles long by twenty-one wide; yet a man can stand in the very middle of it at Mavis Grind and throw a stone into either the North Sea or the Atlantic.

The coastline is crazy. It is a sort of geologic debauch where the rocks seem to have gone mad. They shoot out of the sea in sheer cliffs, spear points and great arches through which one could sail a full-rigged sailing ship. Spotted seals bask on the fantastic red rocks. The great whale blows off shore. Gulls, guillemots, fulmar petrels, shags, and puffins scream from the serrated edges of the cliffs, shoot past in staring flotillas on the tide, and whirl in feathered spray over the onrushing green waves. For six hours each day the Atlantic sets through them, sweeping in great swirling eddies to bring the flood tide. Then it ebbs—and the North Sea races after it, leaping and thrumming through the rips of Yell and Blue Mull Sound. Yet on this fantastic coast is all the colour and beauty of the Shetlands.

Inland is monotony: black peat bogs and the long, lonely moors: the cry of the curlew. There are no streams, only a few gurgling burns which run almost unseen along the black channels they have dug through the peat to empty into shallow, wind-swept lochs, where the water lies black as coffee before the cream is poured in. Drear country, mostly given over to the grazing of sheep; crofting country, where the farmer-fishermen live in little thatched stone huts by the shore, huts crouching, it seems, with their heads down against the sea wind, their thatch held on by old nets and heavy stones. And yet even this desolate inland has its moments of beauty, for the black peat bogs glow purple when the heather is in bloom, and the bare moors have a mosaic of tiny wild flowers . . . if you stoop down to look. And here, mining and counter-mining, are white rabbits, black rabbits, grey rabbits, and just rabbits, in their thousands.

All this is very much as it was before man ever came there. Today you can see a man or a sheep on the Shetland horizon at any distance anywhere he stands against the sky. There is not one natural tree.

As I shivered in the perpetual rain over these wind-swept rocky lochs I began to philosophise about the dourness of life in the Shetlands. I was beginning to wonder whether a man needs to be a philosopher to be a fisherman, or if a certain amount of fishing would not make him a philosopher.

I had been casting automatically and a trout had hooked himself. I fought him. I could not see him, of course, in the coffee-black water. I could just see my thin gut leader cutting the water and then zip under as he made a run. I let him have the line gingerly, feeling him. My rod was bending beautifully, absorbing his tugs; and I could feel each movement of his in my wrist, tele-

graphed along the taut line and slender split cane. I began to tremble a little
—what if I lost him? Was I fighting him too hard? Was this leader any good?
Had I soaked it enough? Had he taken the tail fly or a dropper? If he had taken
the dropper then I was out of luck, because there were some weeds at the
bottom. Ah—what a rush! He must be two or three pounds anyway. . . .

He weighed rather under a pound. But a Shetland brown trout with his
dappled sides and red spots is not to be considered on his ounces—you must
consider his beauty. And I would rather catch a dozen 14-inch trout than one
lazy four-pounder (I don't know whether I am telling the truth or not!);
they fight better, they are athletes, whereas your fat four-pounder is corpulent
and inclined to be sulky. At any rate, that goes for the Shetlands, where loch
trout are small, and your day's catch will invariably average less than half a
pound to the fish. I caught thirty on Eela Water between four in the afternoon
and eight o'clock. They weighed 9¼ lb.—and I have seldom had a finer day's
fishing.

Loch fishing is vastly different from fishing the crystal-clear waters of
British Columbia. It does not pay to strike loch trout; it is better to let them
do the striking. It is a tantalising performance, and a man does just as well to
restrain himself for the fraction of a second until he feels that tiny touch—then
snick him! I do not think that loch trout jump as frequently as the clear-
water fish. You seldom see them when you're fighting them. The water is so
dark that a trout can be barely two inches under the surface; and as long as
he does not turn on his side you cannot see him. That is why, when they do
jump, their revelation is astonishing. You think you have been fighting a
whale—and it is only a game half-pounder. But they are game.

Dull days are best; vile days are better. And it seems as if a day you simply
hate to go out in is perfect. I fished Eela Water on a day dark as pitch, bitter,
raw, with high winds and an occasional rain squall passing over it. I had
seen it first on a bright day from the road, and its ruffled waters seemed to lie
among the green hills like blue silk. But on this day I knew that the water
was brown, with yellow soapsuds of foam among the black rocks—and that
it had not one bit of lee. There was not a place in the loch where I could find
shelter to eat my dinner. The gale seemed to be howling in from both the
North Sea and the Atlantic at the same time. By nine o'clock I was sitting by
a cosy peat fire—dead beat but contented.

We split the trout open, spread them out like a mat, fried them in oatmeal
for breakfast.

There is romance in the Shetland lochs—and great history. One day I fished in the loch of Girlsta—the Geirhildavatan of the Norsemen—where Geirhilda, the daughter of Flokki, was drowned. Flokki was the discoverer of Iceland. And the loch has not changed by so much as one rock since his day. I fished Clousta Loch in a bronze sunset—with the heather in full bloom. It was a little too bright for fish—the air was too clear—but all around me on those rocky hills, waving against the blue sky, the purple heather seemed to be floating in a powdery mist of gold specks. For two years I fished the Shetlands.

At Unst, the last bit of land northward in the British Isles, which I reached by an all-day journey up the islands, with whale-boat, car and motor-boat across two very turbulent sounds, there is an old grey 'great house' still standing, whose gate is made from the two jaw bones of a whale, whose table is old mahogany, heavy with Georgian silver, and where an oil painting of the Duke of Wellington (friend of the long-dead Laird) looks down from the wall. Old herring hulks on the shore give the bare scene the nostalgic quality of an old Victorian steel engraving. It is like an illustration from an old book of our great-grandfather's day. And here, in a deer-stalker cap, disappearing after each lazy breakfast, was perhaps the best sea trout fisherman I ever shall meet. He was a former judge in Mombasa, now the Member of Parliament for the Shetlands. He came back each night with at least a 3- or 4-lb. sea trout—caught among the seaweed-laced rocks of the salt water. When I tried to inveigle him into showing me where he went he refused politely, but firmly: 'That is my secret. I've known this place since I was a boy.'

But the sea trout, though not so plentiful as over in the Hebrides, were my main objective. There was one voe where we tried vainly for sea trout, using chamois imitation sand-eels. It was in the burn tumbling down into this coloured estuary that, after catching several normal sea trout (chiefly on the Peter Ross), I lost two monsters; one, well over eight pounds, which I held on a 3S leader for two hours and forty minutes before my leader simply parted. The thought still makes me squirm, for I could have landed him in the first minute, when he was frightened, had I not, like a fool, stepped back from the bank to give him a longer line. I had him right under me!

The softly waving seaweed forms a brown lace around the rocks of the voe. It waves to you, rising and sinking softly with the long Atlantic swells. The seas foam up white, and run back hastily with little whispering regurgitations, to lie still, so that the white tracery of tiny bubbles fades away, and you look sheer down through blue-green depths to where the shelving black rocks disappear into submarine forests. Then your boat lifts and the seas rush back, and the sea birds cry out. Cliffs rise above, towering overhead to break off in turreted battlements against the rounded clouds. Black ravens sail out of them, hanging in the vast emptiness. The rocks are red, mauve, scarlet. Walls, leaning towers, two-hundred-foot spear-points of red granite.

This was the home of the seals. When we weren't fishing we searched for them among these fantastic red rocks. We came on flotillas of tiny eider ducks, being ushered off by their mothers as fast as they could go. A rare Arctic duck pushed out from his hiding-place, head down, bill stretched out, escaping— he thought—unobserved. Two porpoises curved past, rolling out of the sea and into it again, as if they were perpetually bent like tyres. And they gave sharp, pneumatic little sighs as they went under. At each turn, as we opened up the next red rocky beach or flat shelf, I held my breath at the sight of the seals. There they were, lying on the sheltered slant of these red rocks above a Prussian blue sea. They were buff and dappled with black spots. And when they saw us they were frantic. They had been sleeping head-down with their little black noses towards the sea, and when their leader opened his soft brown eyes, and looked into my face, he nearly went crazy. . . .

Flippity-flap-flip-flop . . . twenty seals hit the water. Gone! You would have thought that the terror which man might have sent into their hearts would have sent them miles out to sea. Not a bit of it. As we heaved there, thrown sky-high on the deep Atlantic swells, the seals came up again; and I tried to stamp that picture forever on my memory. The wild red coast line, the surging blue seas, and around us that fairy circle of seals. They rocked there in the waves. Their dog-like heads stared at us anxiously.

But, even as I have avoided it in this writing, there is another picture I have been trying ever since to forget; that was when the 8-lb. sea trout broke my leader. (He might have been 10 lb.) What happened was that the owner of this burn, the local laird, seeing that it was a gin-clear day, with no sign of a breeze, had offered me, in his generous way, the chance to fish this stretch of water famous for its unusually large sea trout. And I, seeing that it was a gin-clear day, with no breeze, with no hope whatever of catching a big fish— or even any fish that was old enough to know better—put on an ordinary loch leader and started working quite a way up the burn to reach a loch far above me in the soft peat.

This was the home of the seals

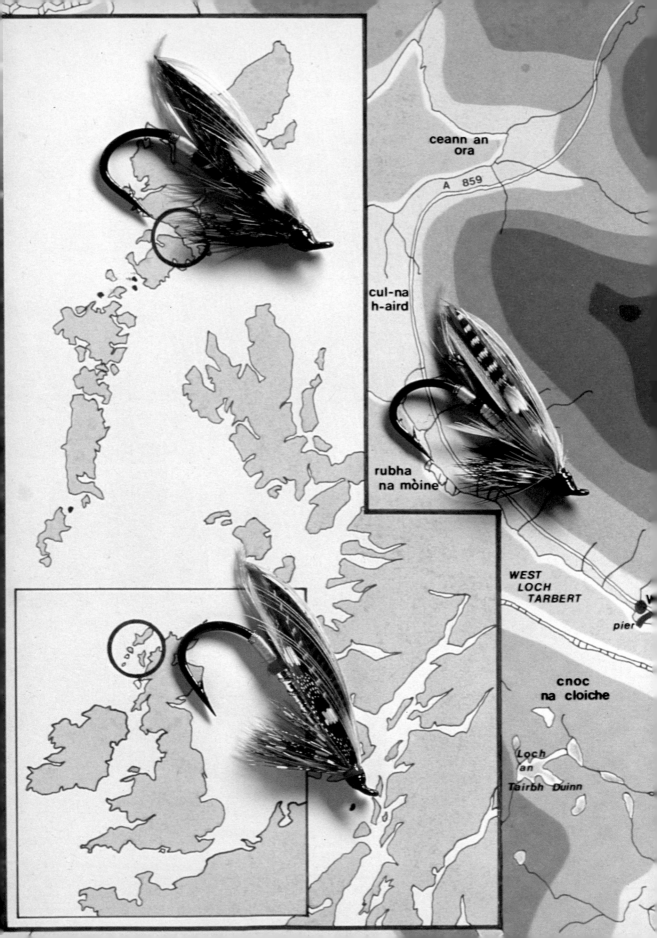

ceann an
ora

A 859

cul-na
h-aird

rubha
na mòine

WEST
LOCH
TARBERT

pier

cnoc
na cloiche

Loch
an
Tairbh Duinn

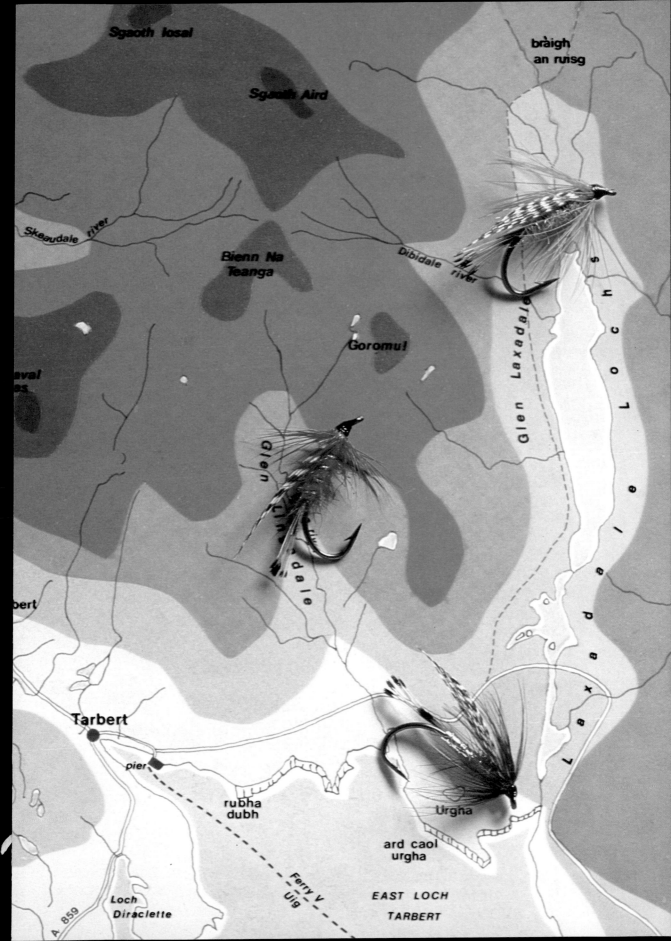

This lonely loch above, with the peat as soft as a sponge around it, was one of the most mournful areas of water I have ever encountered. It gave me melancholia just to look at it. Yet it was to this the big sea trout were migrating.

I had picked up a couple of small sea trout and come to a pool. While I was idly casting from the side of this pool, trying to stir a fairly good fish I had seen in it, and at the same time eat my sandwiches with the other hand, my wife was seated beside me in the hot sun reading a detective story. There was a *whoosh!* and this huge sea trout, whose presence I never suspected, came clear out of water at the foot of the pool. I was so startled I nearly fell in myself.

Then I did everything wrong. I took a few jumps to reach the top of the pool, so as to give me some space to cast, and put my flies over him. On the second cast he took it. I thought he would turn and go down stream. Instead, fast as I stripped in the line to keep it taut, he came right up to me. For an aghast instant he was right below me, his fins and tail working slowly. I could have netted him as easily as you could pick up your hat.

Then I stepped quickly backward up along the burn, to give some more yardage to that dangerously short line—in case he should jump—and he was off!

I persuaded him not to go through some rocks and up a fast slant of water just above me, and he decided himself not to run out of the pool down below. Instead, he just went to the bottom of this pool—and stayed there. I do not think either he or I moved a yard in the next hour. I could work him inch by inch to the surface. But every time my dropper appeared he bored irresistibly down again. So there we were.

As I said, you can see a sheep a mile off anywhere on the skyline of the Shetlands. The bread-van, coming along to deliver some loaves to the laird, stopped on the granite bridge below me, the driver walking up to me to inquire: 'Why don't you pull him up?' I explained the size of the sea trout, my frayed 3X leader, and so on. He went off shaking his head. The news went about over the Shetlands. Two young men appeared from nowhere, leaned over the bridge, watched me silently. An old woman, carrying a creel of peats on her back, knitting as she was walking, also paused on the bridge. They discussed me with each other. I ate the rest of my sandwiches with my free hand, keeping a steady bend on my tip with the other, and my wife poured me out my ration of tea into the top of the thermos flask. I asked her to get some small stones. I threw those down. Nothing stirred him.

'It is a question of patience,' I asserted. 'Which of us tires first.'

Actually, I wanted to break the line. The suspense was getting on my nerves. Therefore, when the laird's factor came along and, in his gruff way, said: 'Why do you no' pull him up?' I complied. I took the line in my left hand below the first guide, held it firmly, and bent the rod. For that was all I did; the big fish never moved. Then the rod straightened out.

'*Lost him?*' gasped the factor.

I just nodded. There was nothing to say.

As we stood there, staring down into the pool, the huge fish jumped and fell on top of the reeds directly opposite us.

'Whooh!' gasped the factor; 'yon's a *big* un!'

He went away, to report to the laird, I suppose, that the foreigner had almost caught one of his famous big sea trout. I trekked wearily home across the island to another laird with whom I was living. For consolation, he at once produced a full whisky bottle.

I came up to the Shetlands the first time to go off in a whale-catcher with Olsen, the dean of the Norwegian gunners. We shot an 80-foot fin whale off the Gulf Stream. But that is another story. What did amuse me on this trip, from a man who had shot 2,600 whales, was to see Olsen go into hysterics when he hauled up a 3-lb. tom cod. We had run out of food and were letting the whaler just drift along the painted coast of the Shetlands while we fished overside. We fished so deep that, with the sudden decrease of pressure, most of the fish we hauled up had their insides blown out of their mouths. It was one of these that Olsen held up for me and the ten other Norwegians to admire.

'Py Golly! how's dat for a big von!' exulted the man who a few days later shot an 80-ton whale.

There was one morning with Olsen which I shall always see. We had stopped our engines, not anchoring, lying near the Gulf Stream. The sunset was in bars of black and gold. Even Olsen was moved, but all he said was: 'Leetle breeze from de nord. . . . ' Then 'Py Yesus! she yust like a voman, dot damn Gulf Stream—never know where the hell she is when you vant her!'

We had been trying to find the Stream as the fin whales go down along it feeding on the plankton, the millions of 'skrimps,' as Olsen called them, which line its flanks.

That night I told Olsen I would not go to bed; I wanted to see the dawn,

I sat on a hatch, staring at the long glistening swells coming across the Atlantic until the seas turned a light silver-blue and a flamingo light glowed behind the mountains of the sky. I watched the sun come over the rim of the world. Then, with no sense of motion, the clouds silently changed shape and seemed to take fire. The seas turned green as polished jade. And all around us were the black fins and tails of hundreds of basking sharks.

Another day had come—and we went westward on our chase of the whale.

The creaking cries of the gulls in Lerwick harbour, like a lot of rusty tackle, are still music in my ears (although I hate the birds); and so are nights in a herring drifter in which I went off while I awaited the chase for whales. We shot about two miles of net off the Skerries as a last slant of sun caught a headland and it blazed like an opal. That midnight the net gleamed in phosphorescent fire, the herrings came in like chips of silver, and huge jelly-fish rolled down the mesh to expand and glow like moons in their submarine world. The gulls swooped down for the fish at dawn, the skuas (the real sea hawk) pursued and made the gulls vomit them in mid-sky; and the sulphur-headed gannets, the solan geese, dropped like plummets into the waves. One of the drifter's crew had been in a trawler at Gallipoli during the last war; he reminisced about it moodily as we sat there through the night—boiling the tea in the fire made to provide steam for the deck winches—and one old Shetlander addressed his crony: 'James Robinson, you and me haven't seen anything of this world. We might as well have been brought up in a barrel.' 'Constantinople,' as they had dubbed their travelled friend, groaned and shut up.

It may sound devious, but there was a hard practicality in the lives of such men, making their sparse livelihoods from it, that made the theoretical, over-technical discussions in comfortable London clubs about just what flies to use; the Spey cast; wet versus dry-fly, etc., seem unsubstantial as a soufflé. I'm not saying that all fly-fishing, yes, even bait-casting, is not a fine art—and I get as much pleasure out of armchair fishing as anyone—but I do think that there are far too many people who are satisfied to accumulate tackle and terminology, rather than to fish. I was fishing behind Kirkcudbright with a sour old gillie when a gentleman came down with a creel that contained about every fly and gadget you could buy in Pall Mall. The loch was also, as I discovered, *his* water! On which he very kindly let me stay: 'There is plenty of room for both of us,' he said generously. Whereat the gillie growled under his breath: 'Yon'll catch no fush . . . his line's out of water all the time.'

It was in the way 'you *present* it to the fish!' said the gillie, that determined the potency of the fly. The other man had earned the gillie's hatred, because he was changing his flies all the time.

Now, what makes a fish take those bunches of feathers tied on a hook? Surely, he can't *always* think it is a fly. Or even a shrimp. There is nothing in Nature like the brilliant, gaudy, tinsel, silk and colour of the best-killing salmon flies. *Something* certainly attracts them; other *Somethings* certainly do not; though why or why not could probably be argued, without getting anywhere, to the end of time. Therefore, when I remember a heated discussion with a friend of mine, a fanatic fisherman, as to just which *four* flies would we carry around the world—if we had to make such a selection—I have to grin. He, I, and two others, in a London club, got all hot and bothered between flies for Scotland versus flies for southern England—Silver Doctor and Peter Ross, say, against the Blue Upright and Tup—so that we almost came to blows. After each being insulted to his elastic limit we agreed, I think, on something like this: Butcher, March Brown, Blue Upright, Red Spinner . . . with everybody demanding a Silver Doctor for a fifth. Or a Greenwell's Glory. Then came the question of size . . .!

Of course we were all fools—as any fisherman will agree. An entomologist would have said we were lunatics.

Now, size, I contended, was one of the most important considerations of all; and, again, fish took bigger flies at night. Were any of these a night fly? The battle began in another ring.

I was fishing Scotland that year—Scourie, the last place up on the north-west coast. And as I drove up from London I planned to stop the night at Dalwhinnie. Lo! who should I see, coming in all bronzed from the loch, but my fanatic fisher-friend? And what did he have in his hand? *Two trolling rods.* Furthermore, his proud gillie, before my friend could silence him, declared that they had an outboard motor to take them up to the head of the lake; that 'the gentleman' had only to place two stones on his line, on that section remaining in the boat; and that, fishing this way, they had just caught a 6-lb. trout!

Even more, it came out, the gentleman came here every year—this 6-pounder was nothing to some of the fish the gentleman had caught—had I not seen some of them mounted in the gentleman's fine house in London (and had I not!) and—they never went fly-fishing!

Now, as I purposely ran the risk of opening this book with talk about coarse fishing, as some people will put it; and as I have given plenty of instances of fish caught on spoon or spinner or with frogs, I can tell this joke about the theoretical fly expert. I daresay my friend could cast a fly like an angel, if he put his hand to it; but his mind was on size, nothing else. Huge fish peered at you from every wall of his fine house in London. Dinner conversation was about nothing else. He *was* a fanatic fisherman, so touchy about it that when I tried to rag him that sunset—asking what four flies he had brought up—the beer itself seemed to become soured by his resentment. My wife and I hurriedly got in our car and drove on another two hours to find a neutral inn to spend the night.

I haven't seen him for years.

Scourie (although it seems hard to believe there could be such a place, even in Scotland) is forty miles from a railroad. That is one attraction. The other is that for both trout and salmon fishing it is about as good a place as you will find in England or Scotland, short of renting a stretch of river for yourself. The one hotel was, at the time I fished there, run by an ex-game warden of the Duke of Sutherland. It was full of retired admirals, colonels, majors, and colonial officials—all cursing the weather.

'This *beastly* sun!' you heard every morning, as another day dawned, windless, fair as any in Eden. How they swore at it! The language those men used!

This was the year of the big drought. No fish had come up. There were some fine trout in the lochs. In one, which could only be reached after a heart-breaking climb, there was a sub-species of trout I have never seen elsewhere. It was lightish, with an almost mauve-coloured back, and very few, but enormous, black spots. Their fighting capacity was equal to a trout about twice their size; and although a lucky 2-pounder was the largest I got I felt these fine trout worth more than twice the climb. This loch had green moorland running away from it; but there was one loch near it whose bleak granite walls seemed as confining as a prison's. I always felt slightly uncomfortable when I fished that place. There was another loch, also high, from which 10-lb. trout were taken, all apparent cannibals with the up-tilted jaws of the

74

ferox. There was a river, but the Duke of Westminster had rented this fine flow up which, despite the drought, sea trout and salmon were daily passing into *his* loch. The fish in the estuaries would touch neither the fly, Devon, nor sand eel; and the small Loch Baddy, on which the hotel had the fishing every alternate day, seemed as fish-less as a bath tub.

For some extraordinary reason of roster regulations in the hotel, I, the last comer, got put on the bottom the first day, then rose to the top for three places after three people who left on the same day. By another coincidence the rains came the night before this. The result of this heavy rain was that we could hear the burns rising to rush down the mountainside. So, when I was asked, having first choice, where I would fish the next morning—I took Loch Baddy.

There is a stiff mount of burn leading up to the loch from the sea, then the stretch of lake, then another stiff burn leading up from it. The rains had abruptly stopped; it was another of those 'beastly' sun-filled days, without a breath of wind. I fished from shortly after nine o'clock in the morning until exactly six p.m. without a rise.

In the meantime, the gillie and I could watch the mountain burn receding. We gauged that by the patch of yellow foam which terminated its swirling path out into the lake. This foam was ever drawing nearer to us. We had beached our skiff and I was just practising—to see how long a line I could keep in the air. Doing this, I heard the *click* as my fly hit against some boulders far behind me. My luck was in, for I reeled in the line and saw I had broken the tip off my hook.

It was a large Thunder and Lightning I had bought over in Ireland, from the old man who ties flies just above where the Corrib flows under the stone bridge in Galway. I put on another exactly like it. I was still practising, trying to hit that patch of foam, and had just said to the gillie: 'There, I've done it,' when he shouted: '*You've got him, Sir!*'

A fine silver salmon came straight out into the air from the foam. I was into him, all right.

The following things happened. Watching the burn recede, it had never occurred to our thick minds that the loch was also falling. And now my salmon, by his run, had signalled that he intended to cross the loch. While we were struggling to get the boat off, the gillie broke an oar. A leap far out made me gasp that I had already lost the fish. Then a dangerous jerk at my rod told me he was still with me. With an oar and a half the gillie tried to get

me somewhere near him, so that I could win back some line in my reel. In
the meantime, because the day had been so gin-clear, I remembered with horror that I had put on a 3X leader. I told this to the gillie, who merely said:
'It's a peety . . . he's a fine fish!'

Then the salmon sulked. He went straight down to the bottom in the
middle of the open loch, the safest place he could have found; and there he
stayed for an hour. I resisted the gillie's advice to 'pull him up'; the memory
of that 8-lb. sea trout in the Shetlands was lived all over again. I kept saying
to myself: 'It's a psychological problem. Get on top of the salmon *mentally;*
don't keep telling yourself that you're going to *lose* him!—keep saying that
you are going to *get* him!'

And so I managed to keep cool and resist all hints of the gillie that it was
time he was getting home to his dinner; did I know he had two miles to
walk to his croft after he left me at the hotel? Yes, I knew. 'Weel . . . ?' I did
not answer. One hour and thirty minutes passed, then another ten minutes—
'Sir,' said the gillie, 'you'll never get him up—not unless you worry him.' I
told him I could feel the fish weakening. And so I could! It is too intangible
a feeling to put into words, but I knew the salmon was tiring; he had been
boring, even if slightly checked, one hour and forty minutes against the bend
of my light trout rod. And foot by foot I worked him up. When he came near
the surface he did not jump, but made one or two runs with his back almost
out. Then he turned for a fraction of a second, showing his side. Then he
began going around slowly in feeble circles. 'Now,' I said firmly to the gillie,
'I'm going to *lead* him past—don't try to row up to him—keep your oar and
a half out of water—*but*, when he comes past—gaff him!'

I brought him past. The gillie defied all the laws of balance by leaning so
far out the boat that only his boots seemed to remain in it—bang, rattle,
bang . . . the salmon was flopping on the floor-boards.

He was a clean fish, with the sea-lice still on him; 14½ lb. Not a giant, I
know; and it took me an hour and fifty-five minutes to land him. But a west-
coast salmon does not run to the size you get them on the east coast. This one
was taken on tackle light for even sizeable sea trout. Anyway, he was mine.
Even the gillie rejoiced, possibly because he knew a good tip would be coming.

And that night an envious admiral, shaking his head at my luck, cor-
dially bought me a drink. 'Dammit all,' he said, 'I'm glad to see *anyone* catch a
salmon!' Which could have been put otherwise.

Two days later I again got the loch. But this time when I came down for

He was a clean fish, with the sea-lice still on him

the boat I saw a man fishing in it out in the middle—and he wore the kilt. 'The Laird's brother!' warned the gillie, hoarsely. Brother be damned, I informed him; this was my day on the loch. So I called out rather rudely. A very polite little Scot rowed ashore—he had no one in the boat but himself—expressed his chagrin that a mistake had been made, but . . . looked enviously both at me and the loch. 'Perhaps,' I suggested, 'you wouldn't mind if we both fished it? I don't.'

'Oh, of course! of course!' he said, 'jump in.'

But he kept the bow seat. And from then on we had a very interesting (and trying) morning. The gillie knew on which side his bread was buttered; I was a stranger, a passing man; this was the Laird's brother. *Ipso facto*, he should have the first cast at every likely beat. So it went. The wind roughened. This time I had on a stout 2X leader. This time I was ready for business. And this time I watched the little major, for that was his rank, *pull* the fly away from a big salmon twice. He just struck at the 'boil'—which doesn't always mean that the salmon has got the fly. Very often a salmon misses. After a final try, for this same fish, when it came out of water with its mouth open, I suggested meekly that I have a turn. The major, reddening (after all, it was only his fanaticism that had made him forget me) said: 'Of course! of course!—Jock, turn the boat round.'

The salmon, thank heaven, was still waiting. He took my Thunder and Lightning on the first cast. Then we drifted all over the lake, in and out among the dangerous rocks—for the wind was very high now—with the major *pushing* a net at him! I can still see his behind in the kilt, with him leaning as far as he could out the bow, shouting back: 'Up, Jock! Up! My God, man . . . ah, there he goes again!'

After fifty minutes of that I again brought the salmon past. 'Gaff him!' I said. He was gaffed. This one was also fresh run, just up, absolute silver—$10\frac{1}{2}$ lb. And the admiral did not buy me a drink that night.

Two days later I got the loch again. By now the drought was in full force again. Any fish that had moved up into the lake had by now, we were sure, gone up the dwindling burn. Nothing stirred. I had taken with me my wife's mother, whose late husband had been an ardent fisherman. She had seen plenty of fly-fishing, but never an American bait-caster at work. She asked me to show it to her.

Now this was the 'Duplex' (combination fly and bait-casting rod) which Hardy had made me from the old Abbey & Imbrie. I took out the two top joints, slid up the aluminum bands, so that the quadruple reel was mounted above my hand; and put in a stiff short tip above the first joint. Then I put on a 2-inch silver and gold flat Devon, told the gillie to row me over not too close to a rim of reeds standing along the shore, and made a cast. Luckily, although the soft braided silk line was still dry, I did not get a back lash. I began reeling in the Devon—and was startled by the heavy thud of a big strike.

I killed a 6-lb. salmon in $8\frac{1}{2}$ minutes. The Devon—sliding up the cast and line and coming back to bang him on the nose—obviously scared a lot of fight out of him. And this time, when I got back to the hotel, and the usual crowd was examining fish laid out on the floor, someone said bitterly: 'And what did you get *that* on?' 'A 2-inch Devon,' I replied.

That night nobody offered me a drink. The hate had set in. So had the drought. One man, the one who had caught most of the previous year's salmon, stayed out all night in order to bring back his waning prestige, with no result. One of these men, a man from Nigeria, whom I saw later in the Café Royal in London that winter, came over to my table with a grin and said: 'You *lucky* blighter! No one got a salmon for the rest of that season!'

Gillies, it does not take you long to discover, need diplomatic but firm handling. The local man always knows more than you do. Also, although he may be clever enough to conceal it, he resents your presence: this 'foreigner' he is taking around. This, despite the fact that most of them could not throw a straight line themselves, that they would use line thick as a rope, anyway; and that there is no more suppleness in their thick wrists than if they were casting with a clothes pole. I do not succumb to the philosophy of the local man.

This youngish gillie I had at Scourie broke the tip of one of my rods (a fine two-piece Hardy) by trying to cast a Devon with it when I was far off, fishing from the opposite bank. In a rocky pool not much larger than the average bathroom, in which we watched four large salmon making up their minds whether they were going to run up or not—he wanted to gaff one. With white bumps being raised on me all over by the klegs my temper was never very sweet. I had noticed that every time we came to a small stone bridge on the way home he always asked me to stop the car, while he went off to look at something under the arch of bridge. One night, when he jumped out of the car, I saw that he had my collapsible gaff in his hand. He ran to the bridge. Before I could stop him I heard a thrashing of water—and a fine 10-lb. salmon lay on the grass.

'I've been watchin' him for days!' he said.

'Now what are you going to do with him?' I asked. 'You can't put him back, you've gaffed him through the stomach.'

'For you,' he said.

'Not me.'

'Well . . . Sir . . .'

'He's your fish,' I said.

Now he was in a pickle, and I enjoyed it. The ex-gamekeeper who ran the inn knew pretty well if one of 'his men,' as he called them, got an illicit salmon or not. Gossip travels fast in those parts. 'You can't throw that fish back; you have ruined it,' I insisted. 'You must take him home. You killed it.'

The gillie glared at me angrily. 'I'll get into trouble,' he growled. I told him he could get into it. 'But I'll tell you what I'll do,' I said. 'You needn't come with me to the hotel. I'll drop you on the way, and you can cut across the hills for home. I'd put that salmon under my shirt.'

The next day he was a subdued gillie—until almost lunch time.

Then there was old Tom, on the Lakes of Killarney. I was living at Flesk Castle with one of the Macgillicuddys whose mountains, the Reeks, are named after this ancient Irish family. Tom was lazy. When I wanted to fish the mouth of the Flesk River he always said it was too early for 'throut' there. Finally, I told the hotel, I would go out without Tom. Next day, when I got down there, I found the boat—but no oars. The hotel said that old Tom owned the oars. I got oars. That afternoon I found the boat—but it had no thole pins. Tom had heard about me getting the oars. So I cut thole pins from a stick of green sapling. Of course, the wind *would* rise and my green thole-pins bent. I slithered all over the lake like this. Then I made Tom take me to the mouth of the Flesk; I brow-beat him into it verbally.

There I got eleven fine trout, all with almost salmon-red flesh from feeding on the plentiful crayfish. Even Tom was enthused.

'Now,' I said, 'what about it being too early in the year? How do you account for these, Tom?'

'Ah . . . shure . . . I've killed throut here meself . . . before St. Patrick's Day!'

And when I said to him one day, looking around the almost unearthly beauty of the Lakes: 'You're lucky, Tom, to live in such a place as this!' he merely sniffed and replied: 'Ah, sur—I see it every day.'

V

*Less than an hour from London; days in the Hebrides; and
Murdo Macdermid*

My job as a newspaper correspondent kept me out of England for the six years before the slump of 1930. For these six years I was not in any one country for over six months—except for a year in Soviet Russia. But this work also brought me into intimate connection with the British Foreign Office; and in there was a man who knew well the Hebrides, which I had fished twice, and who also belonged to a fishing club at Uxbridge, just forty minutes' car drive from London. The last place on earth you would ever think of catching a big fish.

It is a restricted club whose membership, I believe, is largely made up from the Foreign Office. During the May-fly season you may not bring a guest. That is, not with his rod. He may use yours, if you want to be so self-sacrificing, and I was invited to fish there one Saturday afternoon when the May-fly were on. I pleaded an engagement, saying that one of the secretaries from the Russian Embassy had been invited to my home for lunch. 'Get rid of him,' said this Scot from the Foreign Office, 'it's only forty minutes' drive. I'll expect you about three.'

I went. There was a tremendous hatch of fly. But, aside from several grayling (which I had to put back) I did not touch anything. Then I saw my friend calling to me from another branch of the river. I climbed two barbed-wire enclosures and came up to him. He pointed: 'There's been a fish rising under those overhanging blackberry bushes there. I don't know what size he is. Try.'

I did. I must have made about twenty casts, trying to put the fly on the water so that it would float down under the blackberries without any drag. 'That's it,' said my friend, 'that ought to be just over—'

There was a 'sup' and I struck. Instantly we both saw that it was a large fish, a very large one, for that part of the world. 'Net him!' I gasped, as the fish headed straight for a root; 'there's going to be no playing with this one!' I brought him across, my friend skilfully slipped the net under him—a 2½-lb. Rainbow was lying on the bank.

'Well, where on earth did you get *that* one?' came a voice, which happened to belong to the owner of that river, through whose estate it ran; 'that ought to be a record.'

I believe it was. At any rate, it was the most beautifully shaped fish I have ever seen. We all agreed at the club that it was absolutely perfect. It was also, I believe, the record for the club—anyway, you will see it entered in their book. This was Saturday. The trout spent that night and Sunday in the icebox of the St. James' Club. On Monday morning, I took it along to Hardy's. They agreed as to its perfection. They made a cast of it. Today it hangs over my desk.

'It's always the case!' smiled my Foreign Office friend ruefully. 'The passer-by always catches the biggest fish.'

You see, even that 'record' does not make me tell a fish story.

For my long vacations those years I took two September fishings over in the Hebrides, the Outer Isles. Rum, Mull, and Eigg—we passed these in our little steamer. It was the three lochs above Tarbert that we were headed for, in Harris; and, on the second occasion, my quest also led directly to Murdo Macdermid. For here was the prince of all gillies! The perfect companion.

'I don't know what makes the sea trout rise—or what makes them go off so suddenly!' mused stocky, ruddy-faced Murdo Macdermid; 'they puzzle me.'

There are three lochs there that go up like steps. A long shallow one, which the fish reach after an unbelievably steep climb from the sea. A short

The road to Benbecula

round one, with two or three very productive islands in the middle. And then the long, long loch going up between the high bare green hills to the top burn. All three are different. You rotate your beats. And you may not use anything but the fly. No spinners at Tarbert. And every morning when I watched Murdo Macdermid walking down the path along the long loch from his croft I knew that a grand day lay ahead of us—even if the sea trout were perverse.

There was a rise nearly every day of herlings about 12 inches long, some a bit larger, that came on with the suddenness of a cloud passing between you and the sun. Then they would stop. Not a fish. I often thought it was the cloud effects that stopped them. I don't know why yet. But when these were rising you were taking in sea trout just about as fast as you could fight and land them. Mostly on the Peter Ross. Then there would be the long, long row up the right side of the loch, fishing every likely stretch or rocky promontory, for a possible big one.

On one such day, when the wind and rain were lashing the big loch, Murdo Macdermid said: 'I'd try the Teal and Green, Sir. I'll not know why, but I have an *idea* they will fancy that.'

So I took off the reds and put on the Teal and Green—a fly I carried, but had never had much luck with. We fished all the way to the top with never a rise. We saw some big fish, salmon, moving at the mouth of the peaty burn, waiting to move up. And I made a long cast over them. My second or third cast got me into a fish.

Now a most peculiar thing happened. This salmon was not a very big one (he was only 7 lb.); but I simply could not bring him to the top, neither would he jump; but *in* the water he was putting up a furious fight. He had nearly all my line out half a dozen times. And time and again I would get him so close that the top of my cast came out of water—then he always shot down. 'He's a most *peculiar* fish!' said Macdermid.

Then we saw what it was—a small trout had taken my middle fly. This small trout made a horrible fuss over the salmon's head, every time it saw itself being hauled up towards the light surface. This commotion above him, which always happened when the water began to lighten, drove the salmon down.

We fished the islands. On my last day at Tarbert I had arranged for a car to pick me up at the loch and race me to the little steamer, down to which I had already sent my luggage to lie on the wharf. But, as luck would have it, this was the best morning I ever had at Tarbert. I had the lower loch, and already had two above 2 lb. and was into a third, just under 4 lb., when I heard the car squalling at me from the bank. The driver was shouting excitedly and waving his arms. I waved mine, pointed down to where my line was zig-zagging all over the water. 'The boat is leaving!' came the cry. 'You must come!'

Well, it could leave, and be damned to it. I set myself down to another ten minutes' fight, at least—the Klaxon uttering one long perpetual scream now like a dying moan—and I got the fish. Rowing at full speed for shore I took my rods apart as the car raced for the wharf. The steamer was just casting off. My wife was trying to hold it—almost physically, looking back despairingly. When we ran up its gangway and it gave a toot and pushed off, the Captain came along as soon as he got out into open water and was ready to berate me. When he saw the fish he grinned:

'Well . . . perhaps it was worth waiting for that one,' he said.

We fished Uist, getting only one large and blackish salmon, and snipe-shooting there in a high wind I missed more than I care to think about. I was too anxious. Then we got into a cart and crossed the sands and the shallow tide-rip at low tide to fish Benbecula—which is the only way you may get to that island; no steamers stop, and the green waters of the Atlantic raced through our strong wheels up above the hubs.

Mrs. Macaulay's porridge is justly famous on Benbecula. She cooks it all night. Her son, in a kilt, keeps the bar of this lonely, diminutive pub. When he has had some of the stock he will do a sword dance for you. All the boys on this small paradise seemed to be named Charles Edward and the girls Flora MacDonald . . . from the days of the Young Pretender and the original Flora MacDonald who hid him, when he was dressed as a woman. The present girls were called Flora MacDonald to such an extent that they were known in our little hotel as 'Dining-room Flora,' and 'Upstairs Flora' and 'Kitchen Flora.' And what breakfasts those were! with the mushrooms we used to pick and bring in off the turf. Benbecula, for me, did not prove a good trout island. So I waded out at low tide to one of the little adjacent islands, just as the peasants who were growing grain there waded back at sunset, and shot ducks. I shot them lying against a hay-rick, listening to an islander tell me how he could not talk to me—'because you do not know Gaelic!' And when I asked him if he had words for, say, the colour of that far island turning purple in the sunset, he merely laughed: 'I could nae deescribe it to you in English. The language is too weak!'

He knew what to do with my whisky flask, however; and once, when he was passing it back to me, and I dropped it to take a snapshot at a passing duck (which I didn't hit) he stared at the spilt whisky unhappily.

'That was an *awfu'* thing to do!' he said.

At South Uist we went ashore, saw the verandah of the hotel literally paved with sea trout—and were told that the *average* for that year had been $2\frac{1}{2}$ lb.! This was the famous Loch Boisdale, perhaps the finest sea-trout fishing in the British Isles. But we were told we could not fish there; all the beats were taken up.

'What is more,' said the proprietor with almost a sadistic pleasure, 'you'll no' be able to fish here *next* season. I'm all booked up.'

But, strangely enough, it is one place that I have no wish to go back to. The fishing seemed almost a business there. It was too well organised. Still, if you want to be sure of catching masses of fine sea trout, that's the place.

VI

Six wandering years; drives around Ireland—and political fishing; horses over the Caucasus; fishing the headwaters of the Kuban; an English hermit in Moscow; unfriendly frontiers on the Danube

The six years when I was never in any one country for over six months, when I was living in Wagon-Lits and Ritzy or non-Ritzy hotels; when I was arguing with Customs officials, concierges, and foreign chancelleries around the world; when about the only things that ever caught up with me were my bills, were years, you would think, that held little chance for sport. Yet I saw to it that they provided just that thing. I believe that you do not learn much about any country by sitting in its capital—I had been some four months knocking about remote parts of Spain before I went to Madrid to see Primo de Rivera—and fishing with the Shetland drifters or over at Stornoway in the Hebrides taught me much more about the plight of the British herring industry than I could ever have dug out of the Ministry in London. So when I suggested to my paper that it would be a good thing to take my small round-nosed car and drive around the perimeter of Ireland—both the Free State and Ulster—so that Irish in the States might have some first-hand impressions of what it was like these days, my paper, being far-sighted, snapped at it.

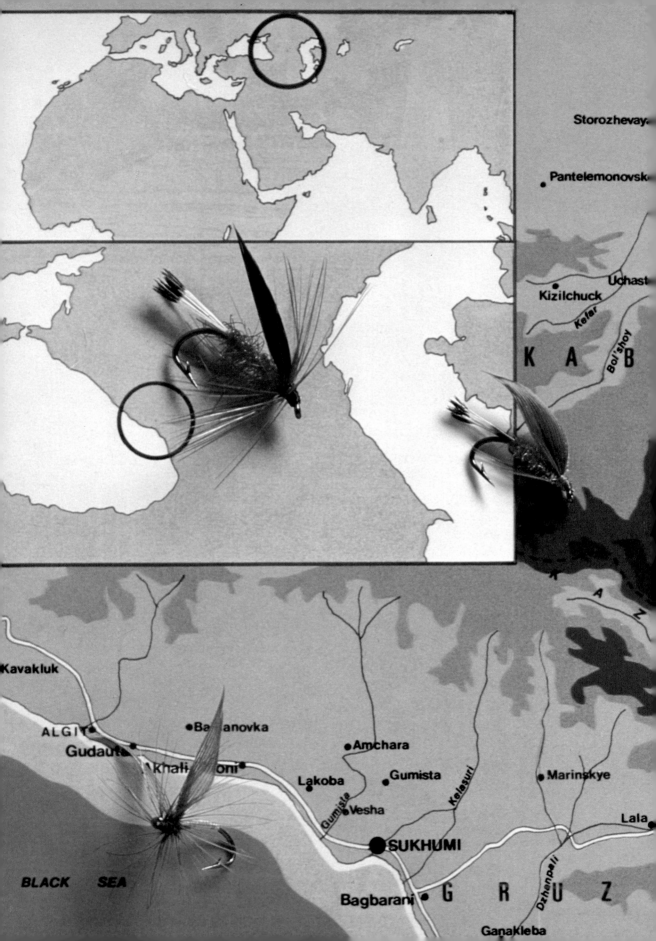

Storozhevay

Pantelemonovsk

Uchast

Kizilchuck

Kelar

Bol'shoy

K A B

A Z

Kavakluk

ALGIT

Gudauta

Banianovka

Akhali Afoni

Amchara

Lakoba

Gumista

Gumista

Marinskye

Vesha

Kelasuri

Lala

SUKHUMI

Dzhenpali

BLACK SEA

Bagbarani

G R U Z

Ganakleba

It was not my fault that the Punchestown races were at Naas; that the Shelbourne in Dublin was full of perhaps the gayest collection of sporting people on earth; that I lost heavily on the races, and, in remorse, left the flesh-pots of Dublin—and poached every stream that I could, driving up the west coast of Ireland. In Connemara and in the Joyce country I got some most useful Irish politics that way. (But I got amazingly few fish!) At Dingle I lay over a few days to go off with the Irish 'nobbies' trawling in Bantry Bay. I lived with the captain of the little *Mary Immaculate*, and at night both he and his wife told me what the big steam trawlers were doing to all the little Irish fishing villages: 'Ruining us, they are!' said Captain O'Flaherty. 'Mind you,' said his wife, 'if it wasn't for the remittances coming back from America—sure Dingle itself wouldn't be here!' All the way out to the fishing grounds in the 'nobby' Old John was down on his knees in our cabin, praying and counting his beads, for luck, and against the physical ordeal that lay ahead of him; for he was an old man, and he hung as if crucified on the warp getting in the trawl. The last day when a fog came down we saw the big grey shape of an Atlantic liner, her horn blowing, feeling her way past through the murk.

It was raining all the time, and the old man at the tiller waited until he got thoroughly drenched before he put on his yellow oilskins. 'Ah,' he said, 'I knew a man that trolled naked. Galway, he was. He took off his clothes and put himself into a bag. It had holes for his arms and legs.'

Commissioned by the *New York Sun*, in 1919, to write some articles on Sinn Fein, I deliberately used my trout rod as a bit of camouflage. At Killarney I got Mr. O'Sullivan, the butcher, to give me the lie of the land; where, in his judgment, was the best place to fish—were there streams handy? He took me out in his car, where he fell into a dissertation about trout.

'A delightful subject!' said Mr. O'Sullivan. 'It holds so many contradictions!'

'Are you one of those men who carry every fly in the world in their book —or do you chance it with just six or seven kinds?' I asked.

Mr. O'Sullivan stopped his car: 'I belong to the latter school. And I'll tell you why . . .'

'Is it true,' I asked, 'that some of the lads were going to ambush a British lorry on its way to the Gap of Dunloe yesterday—only, the British took the wrong road by mistake?'

'Sure! and how the divvle did you hear about that? Mind you now . . . they were only Black and Tans . . . 'twould have been no loss.'

'I think I must have driven right past the lads in ambush?'

'Well, if you took that road yonder to the Gap of Dunloe—you certainly did. They was lying there all day. The British always take the wrong road.'

'I was lucky.'

''Twas not luck! Ye had the Major with ye. Nobody'll touch *him*. And you tell the Major we'll allow none of those Sinn Feiners from Cork to come over and burn down Flesk, either.'

'Suppose you're reserving that burning for youself?'

'Ah, shame on you. The Major's a Unionist—we know that better than he does. But he's no —— absentee. Tell me (suspiciously) I thought you were talking about trout?'

'Personally,' I said quickly, 'I think a 9 ft. 3 in. rod is quite long enough. And a two-piece rod gives you a better action, doesn't it?'

'Ay—that's true. But you'll not be carryin' a two-piece rod about with you in a car.'

'No, you can't carry a two-piece rod about with you in a car. And especially in railway trains! Do the I.R.A. drill much in these parts?'

'I'll be gettin' back now,' said Mr. O'Sullivan; 'it's not trout ye have on your mind at all at all.'

In 1925, when the Rumanians were shocking the world with their organised murdering of the Russians they were inducing to escape across the Dniester (and then shooting them as they crossed the river to Kichenev) I got into Bessarabia without a permit. I lived with some Russian sturgeon fishermen in the frozen marshes of the Danube delta, sleeping in their clay hut on the top of their clay stove. The Russian peasant is outrageously courageous when it comes to talking; he says everything that is on his mind—if it is a complaint—even though he knows he might get killed for it. And I almost had to shut these people up when they began pouring out what they knew about the Tartar Bunar massacre which had just taken place—Bessarabia was a land of terror in those days.

To get them to the stage of intimacy where they would begin to talk I first had to go out to fish sturgeon with them in their black sailing lodka in the choppy yellow waves of the Black Sea. The days were so cold that I thought my spine would become nothing but a strip of ice. They caught the

sturgeon on long lines of bare hooks that lay like a rake before the shallow
entrance of this mouth of the Danube. The sturgeon, feeling his way up along
the bottom, met these obstructive hooks, gave a flip—and the next instant
he was involved in a whirl of hooks—pinioned. With the ice coating the
black skiff these three men pulled a sturgeon almost as big as a man into the
boat. Then they beat him to death with wooden clubs. Remember, the
sturgeon has armour-plated sides and a head hard as a stone, built that way to
meet the rocks of the bottom up which he must travel against the swift cur-
rents. These hooks, made in Norway, had needle-sharp points. With them
flying around my head as the sturgeon flung himself about the skiff, I can
truthfully say I have seldom had a more terrifying experience in my life.

Rumanian sentries, with fixed bayonets—also sharp as needle points—
challenged us from every bit of solid land in the marsh. But it was so bitterly
cold that they did not take their mittens off to examine our papers. A good
thing for me—for I had none.

These persecuted fishermen had to 'sell' all their sturgeon to the Fish Control—a horrible piece of Government graft—and the big one was duly taken
up to the market at Wilkowo; but a smaller one was walking around all that
afternoon, cut up in small pieces, in the fishermen's pockets and down inside
their boots. That night we made a rich, red soup of him; and we all ate it with
the same wooden spoon. It was considered good manners to lick the spoon
clean before you passed it on. We drank the last of my vodka, and they suddenly produced some red wine from a blue tea-pot. The hut steamed. The ice
boomed and cracked in the moonlit marshes. They sailed me down the Black
Sea the next day, where I was arrested at Sulina. But their story had corrob-
orated a story of official terrorism that I had been putting together ever since
I left Bucharest. Later, I wired it from Constantinople—with never a hint of
these courageous sturgeon fishermen. And it was with a satisfied mind, on my
last night with them, that I stretched myself out on their warm stove—to
dream of the mighty sturgeon, feeling his way up the Danube, with his cold
moonstone eyes.

These stories, my newspaper syndicate discovered, were the things people
wanted to read in the United States. They were tired of politicians. So when,
in the winter of 1928-29, I asked if I could ride horseback the next spring
over the Caucasus—my editor snapped at the idea. 'Tell us how people *live*,'
he said.

From my newspaper's point of view the series of articles I had been commissioned to write meant stories of the remote, strange tribes which the
marches of history had left in nearly every valley in the high Caucasus. For
Wicksteed and myself it meant weeks on horseback in the snow-ranged
mountains (it turned out that for three of these weeks we never saw a road);
it meant living on our own wits and resources almost entirely, sleeping under
a tent I had invented, made from a ground sheet and two sleeping-bags,
cooking our own meals, the subjects of no man's caprice, except our own.
'And,' I said to old bearded Wicksteed, 'it means some of those fine Caucasian
snow trout. We should live well, this spring.'

Wicksteed was an Englishman who came out to Soviet Russia in 1924
with the Quaker Relief, when there was that hideous famine along the Volga.
'Wicker' had seen cannibalism. And what he saw in Russia—the great heart
of the Russian people—decided him to make his life there. A good part of
this trip I am now describing can be found in Alexander Wicksteed's book,
Life under the Soviets.

This is a fishing book. I cannot go into the joy of those days in the high
Caucasus. One detail makes it particularly interesting, the fact that the tribes
were so different, even in some adjacent valleys, that a man from one valley
could not be induced to go into the next one. This meant constant changing
for us, getting new relays of horses; and while we would wait, sometimes a
day or two, until we could get two horses to go on again, I always fished the
streams leading down into each valley. They seemed ideal for trout, but for
weeks I never could rise one—and the Abbey & Imbrie rod (this trip was the
death of it) almost caused me to be pushed over a precipice several times when
its stiff, slotted wooden case caught again on some projecting rock as I tried
to ride my horse around some narrow ledges.

The hospitality of primitive people is very similar, and nearly always
spontaneous, the world around. When we were in contact with any tribe
they invariably gave us milk, bread and their tasteless cheese almost as if it
were a customary rite; yet, like the African natives, they disliked eating their
sheep or cattle as these animals were symbols of their owner's wealth, his
position in the world. Primitive people, when you come down to brass tacks,
are much more materialistic and 'capitalist' than in the sophisticated world.
And not being on a vegetarian diet Wicksteed and I bought a sheep every
three days, when we could get one. This we grilled impaled on sticks over
our campfires, using the same methods as the Cossacks and these mountain

men had used for centuries; a chunk of meat, then a chunk of fat, and so on until an entire skewer was stuffed. They call this 'shaslick,' when you buy it in London, although in London they will seldom add the sour cream, which, smeared on the toasting meat, gives it the most appetising tang. But fish we did not get for weeks.

The chief reason was that we trekked through heavy rains; these mountain streams were sluices of greyish water, often carrying good-sized boulders along; and those streams which came down from the glaciers were almost amalgams of water and rock. It is doubtful if a trout could have seen a fly.

Then one sunset we came out on a high spur of mountains where the swift-flowing rivers, the Teberda and the Kuban, meet to form that eventually long lazy river wandering across the Cossack steppes. Mt. Elbruz, 3,000 feet higher than Mt. Blanc, lay behind us, its cone of snow glowing like a living flamingo in the sunset. There were one hundred and twenty miles of unbroken snow and glaciers between its two nipples and Kazbek. And as I sat on my horse my eyes were still filled with the thunder of the previous sunset, the thunder of emotions inside me, when I sat in the saddle and looked along fifty miles of unbroken snows turning all shades of rose and indigo as night came on.

Below me now lay the junction of these two rivers, the Teberda glacial and grey, the Kuban a vivid bottle-green. Where they met they ran in two parallel bands of colour until they fused in a rapid-filled gorge about two miles from where we had come out of the pine forest. I fished this gorge at sunset that night, getting seven trout. By an accident, as it was I who put them on the ashes and embers, using some of our last butter we had bought from a shepherd tribe, they were excellent. I had forgotten them and had let them get slightly crisp. And that night a Cossack, who informed me that his official status was Instructor in Communism, ate one of these, pronounced it marvellous; but said that I was a Capitalist because I used the fly. The worm, he declared, was the only thing to be trusted. And he even volunteered to produce an old 'character' who caught monster-sized fish in these two rivers. He was so much like the local man in either England or the States, always bragging about how *they* caught such whopping big ones, that he could not understand my frequent fits of laughter. Besides, it turned out that he had never seen a fly. Even more, he did not believe I had caught trout on such a thing. His doubts were dispelled only by my showing him my outfit, wherein

One sunset we came out on a high spur of mountains

there was not a hook which did not have these coloured feathers attached. Still he was dubious.

There was a Turco-Tartar village here, named Utsch-Khalan, at which our man with the two horses saw fit to desert us. He and the horses were just not there the next morning. I left it to Wicksteed to go some ten miles up the valley to get us two new ones. I intended to fish. Working upstream I fished all that morning in the most likely places and never rose a fish. I changed flies, I changed tactics, I fished open water in the slow reaches and behind every rock in the swift. I might as well have been casting in a bathtub. I was eating my lunch, sitting on the bank, with a large slab of black bread with another slab of cheese planked on it, and at the same time idly casting a short line into the swift, sun-dappled river flowing past, when I got a rise. It was so unexpected that I dropped my sandwich in the stream and made another cast over the spot without getting up. This cast brought me a beautiful little trout of about a third of a pound. As trout usually take their colouring from the bottom and colour conditions of the stream, this one's back was a vivid apple green and his hundreds of small spots were a bright scarlet. I then discovered that I had nothing to put him in; as if half-suspecting that I would get no fish I had not taken my canvas fish-bag along.

I got thirty-five trout that afternoon—the greatest number in any one day I have ever caught. I do not think I would have caught so many then had it not been for my argument with the Communist the previous night; I wanted to kill him dead with an unanswerable argument. I found out that instead of the wide, open stretches of fairly deep water, all the fish seemed to be lying in the white water, behind every lee of rock or ridge. I would dump those which I had caught out on the bank, wade out into the river and fish every likely rock. I also discovered that they had a passion for a little orange-and-green-bodied fly, with an inconspicuous wing—neither teal nor grouse nor mallard—that I had always had in my book, but whose name I did not even know, nor could I remember where I had ever come by them. Anyway, I had almost a dozen. And when I found that the trout liked these best I took off the two other flies and fished with these 'United Irelands,' as I found out later they were called. It was an unorthodox, bold gesture, but it resulted twice that day in my catching three fish at one time. I have never had more than two on before or since. With three fish I did not know how to land them; which one should I net? My solution, and I am ready to admit that it was possibly not the right one, was to play them as long as I felt safe, then work them towards the shallow lee of a pebbled spit, drag the top fish up on the bank, slip the net under the middle one—and trust that the tail trout was not rubbed off as I pulled the trio ashore. In both cases it worked.

From that day one particular stretch of this swift green river lingers in my memory. It was where a pine had fallen some years back into the stream. Time and the freshet had turned it round and washed it diagonally out into the river. But its roots had held its butt to the bank, thus causing sand and small boulders to deposit behind it, as they do in those jetties that are built to stop shore erosion. This had made a pool about thirty yards long. It was in this long pool that I caught both of these triple-catches. I took eleven of my thirty-five trout out of that pool alone.

While I was fishing I did not notice that two Caucasians had come out of the forest, on their tiny, cat-footed horses, and were watching me. Their sporting instinct had been aroused. They dismounted, like cats themselves, and walked to the river. Then I saw them for the first time and waved them back. That, too, struck them as being peculiar; it had never occurred to them before that fish could see them. In fact, I doubt if they had ever held a fish in their hands. Then when I was unhooking a fish, they saw the flies! Now, this *was* magic, according to their way of thinking; they could not believe what I then actually showed them—a trout rising to the fly. They began to laugh like schoolboys. They became so excited that they pressed forward to the river again. I could not speak to them as their dialect was not even Russian at its base. But they then appointed themselves my unofficial gillies, carrying my net—heavy and bulging by now—through the thick underbrush from pool to pool, from rapid to rapid, and up each unfishable racing slant of white water. I pulled one of the feathered hooks against a calloused forefinger of each of them and gave it a tug. They yelled with delight when they saw the tiny hook fixed in them. An eagle seemed to add to their surprise and curiosity as he spread his pinions over our heads and then dropped with a jerk onto a dead branch across the stream.

That night, as I had been unthinkingly fishing upstream all afternoon, without ever thinking of how far away I was getting from the village, I was almost two hours finding my way down the dim trail in the dark. When I got to the board shacks of Utsch-Khalan I dropped in at the local wine shop and bought two bottles of that purple, heavy Caucasian wine known as **Naperiouli**. In the shop I found the Instructor in Communism and held up to him the bulging net of fish. I invited him to come to the new schoolhouse, built by the Soviets, and on whose floor I was now sleeping, to share the feast. Wicksteed I found waiting for me, and very hungry. I showed him the trout.

'Good Lord!' said this old hermit philosopher (he was a great Shakespeare and Dante student), 'for once I shall have more trout than I can eat. I have always been a poor man, you know. I have *never* had enough trout.'

Well, he would tonight, I told him; and I suggested that I was going out to lie in the stream, clinging on to a boulder, to freshen me up. I was dog-tired. Hanging there, like a waving flag, to the tip of a boulder sticking up from the racing river, I regained strength and an appetite that would mean the end of all those thirty-five firm trout that came to my share. I informed Wicker, who really knew nothing whatever about trout, that this catch was a memorable one, that I would probably never again have such a day's luck, and that he must not be misled into thinking I was going to repeat the performance. I could see he was having dreams of trout for dinner every night.

Well, supporting that conceited but likeable Don Cossack in his Communist arguments about fishing had been a pug-nosed young schoolmistress, also a Cossack, whom the Bolshies had sent into these mountains to instruct the Turco-Tartar children, and their parents, in the ideology of the Soviets. She, too, seemed to know the answer to nearly everything. But she didn't know how to cook fish—not trout.

At the first bite the face of Wicksteed contracted as if he had bitten an unripe persimmon. Then he rushed for the door. He tried again, took another nibble, rushed out again. 'Perfectly ghastly!' he said.

They were. The Instructress in Communism had cooked them in sun-flower-seed oil. Not only that, she had placed the whole thirty-five in *cold* sunflower-seed oil to let them soak! I discovered that when I rushed out into the kitchen.

'*Nu Vot!*'' said the Don Cossack comfortably—and he and she ate the whole lot. Poor Wicksteed died later in his one room in a congested Moscow tenement. He never did have all the trout he wanted to eat. Also, and I never knew how it happened, I found the tip of my rod broken in the morning. I think the Instructor in Communism had been showing some of the Turco-Tartars how to catch fish with a fly.

Between Yugoslavia and Bulgaria, years before, I made firm friends with the lovable, sturdy Serbs by going out fishing in mid-Danube with the

Frontier Guards. I had just been shot at a few days before, by the Bulgarians, as my yawl, the *Flame*, came down in the middle of the river in what was supposed to be an 'international' channel. They had never seen a boat like mine on the Danube before (neither had anyone else), so they shot at me. Fishing with the Serbs, who loathed the Bulgars, this was the constant joke of our profitable afternoon. 'But what if they had hit you!' roared the Serbs. 'Wouldn't that have been a good joke on them!' Not on them, I replied.

I had been trying to get some stories of the constant unofficial battles along this troubled frontier, but until that day I had never had any success. The local Serbian police were not much better than the Bulgarian—or, for that matter, any police; they were clothed in suspicion. But the minute I hauled up my first sterlet (a minute model of the real sturgeon) we were all brothers at once—and at once one of the Frontier Guards in our skiff began to tell fish stories that made his comrades blush for shame. I told them a few myself. We turned to the bottles of *sliwowitz*, their fiery brandy made from blue plums, and before very long I had to force myself not to take mental notes; they were telling fish-stories even about Bulgarian atrocities.

That night when I came back aboard the *Flame* I told my wife, who was with me on that trip, that I had more information than I dared think about, certainly more than I would dare to use. But I did have three of the finest-tasting fish in Europe, for the little sterlet, a fish with no spine, is one of the daintiest fish in the world, if you boil him and serve him up with a cream sauce.

It is a sorry thing to have to admit, but in that eight months when I took the *Flame* from the North to the Black Sea, these three little sterlet were the only fish I caught in thousands of miles. My trout rods, lashed under the carlines of our cabin, were never put together. We lived on wild ducks in the wilderness of the Rumanian swamps. But if you have ever tried to cook a duck on a Primus stove, you will know how unappetising they were. Usually we semi-boiled them in pieces, then finished them off in a highly seasoned casserole. On the last stretch we were always racing against the lower Danube, off Galatz, freezing over. The trout rods were not used until we reached England the next spring.

VII

Four countries in one year: Chile, England, France and Norway;
Rainbow trout before the volcano of Chillan;
over the Andes; an exiled Dictator

There was one year when I fished four countries: Chile, England, France, and Norway. This was in 1937, at the end of which the Norwegians asked me to write the fishing chapter in their Sports Club year book. It was a pleasant compliment from a race which I greatly admire. And another Scandinavian to whom I loaned the book liked it so much I have not been able to get it back from him since.

Chile is one of the most sporting countries in the world. The Chileans themselves are quite possibly its finest horsemen; they come as close to being Centaurs as modern man and horse can get—at any rate, when you see them riding either on hacienda or at one of their famous horse shows both man and horse seem made of one piece, with one brain and with one synchronised system of muscles; and an American cavalry team with which I went down to Valparaiso told me after the competition that they had never seen such horsemen in their life. This was from men of the famous U.S.A. cavalry school at Fort Riley, at least one of whom had jumped at Olympia. There is a legend that when the Spaniards first landed on the coast in their conquest of Peru, the Indians (who had never seen a horse) fled in terror because they thought both horse and man were one—were monsters—until one Conquistador was knocked off his horse . . . and the Indians attacked.

But it was an Irishman who introduced fishing into Chile—its magnificent Rainbow trout. I saw quite a lot of him in Valparaiso; a big, genial, grey-haired man who had been honorary game warden for the country (self-appointed, I believe), patron of both the horse racing and the famous shows; who, twenty-five years before, had hit on the idea of introducing some Rainbow trout into the swift, green, rapid-streaked rivers that flow down from the Southern Andes. The result has been a miracle. These streams are simply crawling with crayfish—and a Rainbow likes nothing better; until within even the last few years some of them were never fished; and the Rainbow (with that predilection of theirs for travel) have spread all over the country. They might not reach the size of those prodigious Rainbow of New Zealand, but if for fitness and fighting quality they may have their equals, I doubt if finer Rainbow can be found anywhere else in the world.

The result of this is that in Valparaiso and Santiago you find colonies of Irish, English, Scots, and Americans—men from the old nitrate days or the modern copper mines—who, almost the minute they have met you, take you to their homes and show you their rods and tackle, produce a whisky bottle, and in a few minutes are telling you fish stories that make even you blush to listen.

The funny part of it is, they are true. One Naval Attaché said to me, 'When I wrote home and told my friends that the first four Rainbows I caught in Chile averaged over 6 lb., they wrote back and called me a liar!' I merely nodded my head—for, only a few days previously at a strange shoot arranged for the Diplomatic Corps on the hitherto preserved lakes supplying the water to Valparaiso, I had seen this same man kill 48 ducks in one morning, shooting through a hole in a blind (which I had in the afternoon) with only a 20-bore shotgun. It was even said that his country had appointed him to Chile in particular simply because its State Department knew his passion and skill with both rod and gun would make him a success with the sporting Chileans.

He was one.

There is a Scot in Valparaiso, the third generation of his family to be born in the country, who is reputed to be the best fly-fisherman in Chile. He came into my room in the hospital where I was lying, introduced himself, and said: 'When you get out of here I am going to give you some fishing that will take the hair off your head.' The Naval Attaché whom I have just mentioned assured me that this was only the bare truth. And the ambassador of my own country (a fanatic fisherman himself) gave me four of the best and biggest Silver Doctors in his book. 'You will need plenty of backing on the river where that man is going to take you!' he warned me. When I told him the size of my two reels and the weight of the rod he closed his eyes and said: 'Well, then, there's no use going. They'll just run away from you . . . take the lot!'

It didn't sound promising. But I was used to this rod and thought it was better to stick to the devil I knew rather than accept one of the longer and more powerful rods which the Scot tried to lend me. Also, going off with such a reputedly fine fisherman I did not want to take the chance of performing with a rod that might make me look clumsy. So a few nights later he and I, and an English ex-naval officer (who had been in the Secret Service in Chile during the last war), were in a train for southern Chile—for Chillan, the town which was literally wiped off the map by an earthquake a few years later. From Chillan we drove the next day, some forty or fifty miles, I think, to a little village between us and the far, blue, broken silhouette of the Andes. After that there was nothing between us and the mountains but a grim plain of low scrub, roadless and rocky. When the next morning we forced the unfortunate car we had procured through this sea of low undergrowth we passed an occasional horseman who, in this setting, brought back pictures of remote Spain. For he sat his horse with the same idle arrogance; he wore a flat black hat, such as you will see in Andalusia; he was Spanish (with possibly a dash of Indian blood); and about the only essential outward difference was that *this* man held his hat to his head by a strap that was tied to his nose! There is a little black tippet dangling from it that always makes you think these Chilean caballeros' noses must be bleeding. The one or two horsemen we met merely gave us a solemn nod, by way of salute; but an old hag that we came on, a withered old ancient riding side-saddle, cackled at us when she watched us get out of the car and put our slender rods together by the banks of the racing river. The blue Andes never seemed to have come any nearer; they lay always like a jagged line of broken blue glass along the eastern sky.

What made it even more strange was that the volcano of Chillan, on our left, was erupting every ten minutes. So regularly that you could set your

They come as close to being Centaurs as modern man and horse can get

watch by it, it shot a 2,000-foot feather of sulphur yellow into the blue sky every ten minutes. And three times when I had on my first fish I saw that feather shoot up.

This river was the Laja, racing down from the extinct volcano of Antuco in the far Andes. In the long flat sweeps it was a deep bottle-green . . . but swirling. Then it crashed through the rocks it had rounded through the ages, poured white over ledges, and emitted the continuous low roar of broken water. I remembered what the ambassador had told me in Santiago—'plenty of backing on your line'—and my heart sank.

At any rate, I told myself, put on the biggest leader you've got (it was a 2X), soak it well . . . and trust to heaven. It was well I did.

I had picked the side of a broad stretch of white falls where the main river swept past in frothing white water and where there was a lee of green water lying along the main current. I felt that if there were any big trout, waiting for something to come down, this was where they would be. It was easy casting, for there was no high brush behind me, and I kept as long a line as I could in the air, hoping to reach the edge of the white water. I think I must have been even more shocked than the fish when, on my very first cast, just as my fly was sweeping down about opposite me, I got that driving pull of a heavy strike. It was the first cast I made in Chile—and it was the best fish.

Without waiting for any more argument he went straight on down the river, sweeping through the white water, where he seemed to rest, or sulk, for a moment in the green water on the other side. It was lucky for me that he did; practically every foot of my line had been taken out. So there we were. I could not get across to him. Neither could I get him across to me. So I gave him the bend of the rod while I stood there and thought about it.

In these parts of Chile there is a very poor brand of peasant, which exists heaven knows how; they come about as close to living without any visible means of support as you would think man could get. There was the brush-board-and-thatched hovel of one of these ramshackle humans behind me now. Its inhabitants had evidently been watching me for some time. Now, seeing me standing there, apparently doing nothing, a small urchin impelled by curiosity came cautiously up to see what I was doing. We spoke no language in which we could communicate with each other; and when I unhooked my landing-net and snapped it open he almost fainted from fright. But he was a quick-witted little fellow, and, somehow, he comprehended what a net was. I made him take it from me.

So there were two of us standing there now. The fish had remained exactly where he was. I gave him a slow pull. The next instant the fish was going down along his side of the river and the boy and I were stumbling down along the boulders on ours. As I said, these strange, volcanic rocks had been rounded by time, and a more tricky, stumbling, infuriating river journey I have seldom made. For I was deep in the river by now, getting as close to the fish as I could get in order to win back some more line. In this fashion I took several yards back from him. Then I reached a high stretch of bank where the water was too deep, and so came back to land. It was now, I said gloomily to myself, that I would lose this fish. I remembered the big sea trout I had had on for two hours and forty minutes, in the Shetlands. Here was to be another broken heart; for, some fifty yards below me, shone a long sloping shelf of white water in the mid-day sun.

Then the fish took it into his head to command operations. To my confused delight and dismay he came directly at me across the white water, so fast that I could barely strip in the line. I had no chance to reel in. Then he went on up the river, taking the line with him as fast as I could pay it out without fouling it. Then, boring against the line, as if he meant to jump the low falls, he again remained stationary over one spot.

This was exactly what the doctor ordered. I could not have asked him to do anything nicer. Reeling in as swiftly as I could, I worked my way up to him. So there, plus one Chilean boy, we were exactly where we had started over twenty minutes before. I knew it was twenty minutes, because twice during our tussle, I had seen Chillan erupt. That 2,000-foot sulphurous jet!

Now began one of the most beautiful battles I have ever experienced. For I had plenty of line in hand now; when he came past I gave him the bend of the rod for all I thought it could stand—determined he should never cross to the other side of that white water again. And every time I checked him. The green water was so glass-clear that when he swung in the swirls sluicing past me the sun caught and reflected the pinkish stripe along his strong sides. I could watch him fighting the hook. And then he spun in the sun, jumping. He was the very essence of fight. Furious, I think—still not frightened.

There is no doubt that in the ingredients of a fisherman's delight there is nothing comparable to being able to watch a fish fight like this. For I could see him, or his shape, nearly all the time. Chillan erupted once more.

But by now my gallant Rainbow was a slow-moving, sullen thing. His tail working heavily, he lay in the green water about twenty yards out from me. And I looked around for the lee of some rocks and slowly worked him in. I had him in a pool. It was almost still water. He was almost resting against the hook. And then, as the bank was high, and I was an idiot, I signalled the little Chilean boy to wade out and slip the net under him. . . .

The boy did. He was an eager boy . . . so eager that he stabbed the net at the fish . . . pushed him with it! Then he tried to scoop him in from the tail. . . . I jumped. As I did, the boy actually got the fish into the net. I seized boy, net, fish, all at the same time, and threw them all up on the bank. There I dived on the fish.

It all goes to prove the hysterical condition into which some fishermen will get themselves. For this Rainbow was not much over 6 lb. But he was such a beautiful one! That was the point; that small nose, and those deep shoulders, and those firm fighting flanks. This fish had been living in clean water on crayfish galore. I sat on the bank and looked at him for nearly twenty minutes. I had him.

Then I sighed, got up, and went to fishing again.

I got three more fish that afternoon. The next one was a 5½-pounder. He put up a grand fight. But it was not the same thrill. I felt braver now; I could afford to be more rough with them. I could take time out to watch . . . this great river sweeping down in the sun below me. I noticed that on nearly all the flat rocks were the crushed shells of crayfish. Eaten there by some form of bird, obviously. And then, as I was fishing one point, a flock of reddish duck came round it so swiftly they almost swept into me. The Scot, that beautiful fly-caster (and he certainly was one!) had taken one look at my 6-pounder, and immediately set off down river—determined to catch a bigger one. The English ex-naval officer had also examined it. 'Ah,' was all he said. Then he went up the river and began fishing furiously below another fall.

Meantime, I caught two more 3-pounders.

I suddenly became aware that I was very fatigued (for I have one leg which is not quite so good as the other), and I hooked the faithful fly into the cork handle of my rod, tipped the little Chilean brat, and worked back to the car. There I found the Scot and the Englishman, who held the bottle out to me. . . .

'Funny, isn't it,' smiled the Englishman as I wiped my lips, 'how damned *good* it tastes after a day like this! Nothing like the same taste in a city. . . .'

'Ah . . .,' I said—and looked eagerly at their catch.

They were all spread out on the grey boulders. We each had four fish. And I had the biggest. 'It's been a grand day!' I said comfortably.

That ride home, when you're tired—that's another one of the delights of a day's fishing. We could rest in the car. The whisky gave a certain romanticism to our conversation. 'And they feed you well at this pub,' said the Scot; 'we've taught these people how to cook—we'll probably have some duck tonight.'

'But what about the *Rainbows*?' I gasped.

They smiled at me pityingly. The Rainbows, their smiles indicated, would be cooked for me in due course, and in the correct manner. In the meantime we drove through the little Spanish-like village as night came down, dragged off our heavy waders, had a good sponge bath in a clay room off the patio, and got into fresh, light clothes. On our way out to where the buckets of cool water awaited us we passed through the kitchen—and there I saw two fat Spanish-looking women splitting our trout, and hanging them on hooks (like shirts to be dried!) above the clay stove. My big one was being cut into sections for immediate boiling.

The next morning we had him—with a bottle of that splendid Chilean Hock—cold for breakfast. It was the sybaritish send-off for another day of the most splendid fishing.

But on this day I disgraced myself. I not only caught another $5\frac{1}{2}$-pounder, but I also caught the most fish. I led by one. And this one, I was made to feel, should never have been taken. The Scot looked grim.

'What!' I cried. 'You mean to tell me that you throw back $2\frac{1}{2}$-pounders?'

They merely nodded. The implication was that in order to beat them I had taken a fish undersize. I then told them that truly they had taken the hair off my head—as I would off any fisherman to whom I tried to tell this story.

I must admit that a bottle of good white wine for breakfast is not quite the accepted way to start off a day's fishing. Yet there is the stirrup cup, and the hunting breakfast—not altogether a dry one—and there was a vigorousness in the wild Chilean scene, with the blue thunder of the Andes always in your consciousness, that made such a breakfast just right. My objection to drink (in connection with fishing) is that I know of no other sport where the

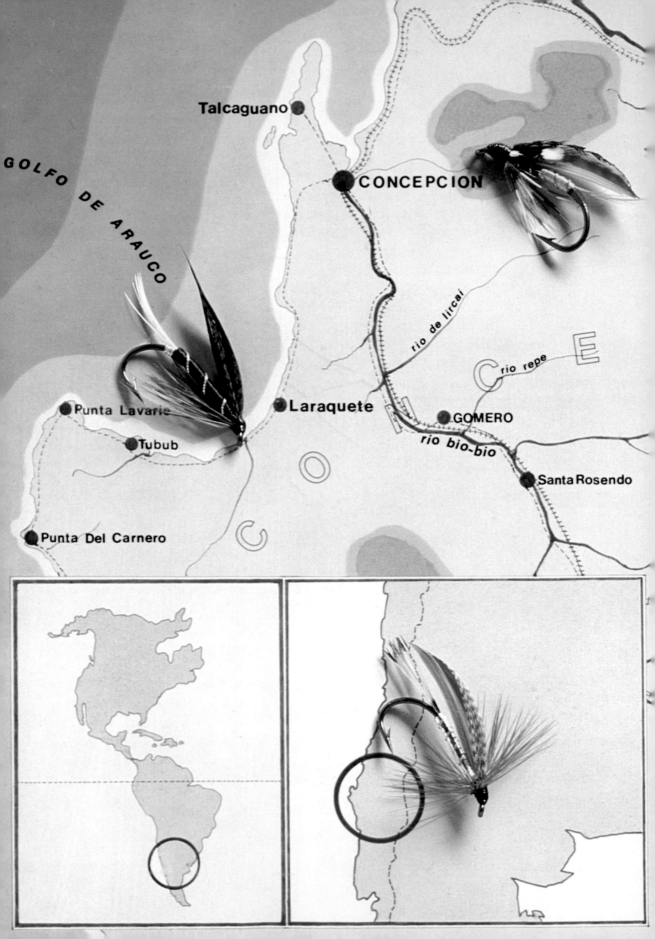

GOLFO DE ARAUCO

Talcaguano

CONCEPCION

rio de lircai

rio repe

Punta Lavarie

Tubub

Laraquete

GOMERO

rio bio-bio

Santa Rosendo

Punta Del Carnero

slightest befuzzlement has such disastrous results. I don't mean merely that you will almost certainly hook yourself, but as the whole art of fly-casting consists in knowing—in your subconscious mind—exactly where the fly is, even when it is behind you, you need a head clear as crystal to know what you are about. I know. I have fished after too good a lunch at a river inn, and had the whole afternoon spoiled for me. I didn't enjoy it. The loveliness of running water was dulled, the leaves lost their sheen . . . and some stretches of water up which I would have waded with delight on a fresh morning . . . now looked too hard to fish.

That is an unorthodox discussion, but this is an unorthodox book. I must admit my two companions did not like the white wine idea; that was mine. But they had even wilder ideas.

For instance, on our return after the second day's fishing—when I brought in that measly little 2½-lb. Rainbow—the Scot was told something that plunged him into a desperate mood.

'It's no use,' he growled to the Englishman as we were eating our dinner (baked trout this time). 'We've got to clear out!'

When I asked what catastrophe had happened to their miraculous strip of river, it turned out that the Scot had just been told that an Indian had reported he had seen another man fishing about ten miles down. Ten miles, mind you.

'Yes, it's too crowded,' they agreed in chorus.

'That's the trouble,' continued the Scot. 'Find a good river . . . go back to Santiago . . . and just *mention* what you've caught on it—and they come down after you like a flock of damn' gulls!'

They had intended to put up a shack on this lonely stretch of the Laja: this horse-country of arrogant Chileans with their hats held on by nose straps. To me it seemed about as barren and barbaric a bit of country as one could wish.

'But now,' said the Scot, 'we are going to try further up. After you go . . . Jack and I are going to try another river I know of in the Andes.'

And so I left them, they going off across the scrub country where Chillan was shooting its yellow jet into the cloudless sky, I, to go down to the snow-capped volcanoes of the lake country and cross a pass into Patagonia—but, in those lakes, I was to catch three of the weirdest fish I have ever come upon.

Down to the snow-capped volcanoes of the lake country

Although over one-fifth of all the developed land in Chile is owned by British subjects, and over ninety per cent of the great sheep ranches are run by Britishers (mostly Scots), there are three great lakes in southern Chile that are (or were) more violently German than anything you could find in Bavaria. Their country, too, is astonishingly like the *bergenland;* only, the towering, snow-capped mountains around you are (you hope) extinct volcanoes. It is terrific scenery where, when I was there in 1936, you could still see the Germans cutting their big farms out of deep virgin forests. The captain and crew of every little ship that took you across the three lakes—Lake Llanquihue is 200 square miles—wore a swastika; you were 'Heiled!' to fury at each wharf you touched; and every little wooden chalet where you slept the night had a sacred room reserved for the *Deutsche Klub.*

I crossed through here, taking the passes of the Andes, hoping to get over to San Carlos de Bariloche in Patagonia. It took several days by boat and car over the high passes to get over to railhead in the Argentine—but I took longer as I rested at the end of one of these unspoilt-by-man lakes to recuperate from too many weeks at high altitudes in the northern Andes. It was at the end of one of these mountain lakes where there is a little Swiss chalet, with real Swiss behind the desk dressed like Rudolph Valentinos— and where even the birds seemed to wear swastikas—that, in a pique, a friend and I locked the President of the German Club in his club for the night.

This we accomplished very simply by stating late at night, when just the three of us were arguing with the Herr President, that we had to go out of the room for a moment. Then, going out, we removed the key from inside the door, locked it from the outside—and went up to sleep.

As I told you, each hotel always had this sacred room for the *Deutsche Klub*. And from this room, about an hour after we had left it, came a roaring that Wotan himself would have envied—he was of a very walrus-like build, this tusk-whiskered President—and he kept up this heavy chant until about three in the morning when some frightened Swiss awoke, realised that this loud noise was not just the usual singing that sometimes came from the *Deutsche Klub*, found a ladder—and released the Herr President. He was very angry.

We had been talking about fish, or, to be more explicit, about fishing; to be perfectly frank, it was about *my* fishing. Although our argument had not begun on such an amicable subject, it was things which he said about my country, about Britain—and about what his crowd was going to do to both of us—which elicited some objections on my part. In fact, the Herr President dismissed the one or two Germans remaining in the Klub, so that he could talk to me privately. Then he demanded:

'What are *you* doing here?'

'Fishing,' I said.

'*Ach so!*' he said shrewdly—'and for what?'

'I don't know,' I replied.

'Ah-ha! You don't *know?*'

'No,' I said. 'I hear there's a very queer type of fish in this lake. It's said to be found nowhere else in the world. What is it?'

'*Ach so!*' he said, triumphantly. 'So the gentleman is *fishing!*'

It was then that I said I had to leave the room for a moment. . . . And we locked him in.

Now I don't know what the name of this fish is. Many readers of this book will, I am sure. But it is spotted like a trout, fights like a trout—has no adipose fin, so of course does not belong to the trout and salmon families—and, if my memory does not play me a dirty trick, I *think* it had no backbone—just a mucilaginous cord, like that of a sturgeon. I may be wrong on that point. Anyway, it was worth catching.

One of the advantages of this 'Duplex' rod that Hardy made me is that you can give a fish nearly everything. It allows you to experiment. And, incidentally, that is another adventure in fishing. Perhaps the greatest. So, when the President and I met about noon the next day, he had a stein of beer in his hand while mine held the little unbreakable aluminum case containing my Duplex. We bowed stiffly.

There was a beautiful river emptying out into the lake across from the hotel. It came down from the Andes in torrents, then flattened out in the boulder-strewn alpine meadow we were in, then spread out fan-wise in a broad mouth to flow quietly into the lonely lake. It was about as lovely a spot to fish in as any man could wish for. The fish, whatever its name was, would, I felt, be lying along the bars off that mouth—waiting in the food stream. And there, again, comes another adventure in fishing: calculating where they are—knowing 'fish water.'

I had an old, heavy, battered 'Phantom' Devon in my bag with which I had never had any luck. It was weary and worn. Most of its paint had come off out in British Columbia way back in 1921; I had tried it in one or two other places; I felt that, really, this Devon should have been long since thrown away; it was a time-waster. Still, it had a personality, with its heavy, sullen head, and revolving body.

So I turned the Duplex into a bait-casting rod, stuck on the Pflueger reel, put on an old twisted wire trace—and this degenerate Devon. The Araucanian Indian rowing my boat came from a race which even the mighty Conquestadores never subdued, nor even the Spaniards who followed them. Their chief characteristic, particularly this one's, is an idol-like, almost God-like dignity and poker-face. His eyes opened a bit when he saw me adjusting all this tackle. But he nearly fell out of the boat when he saw the Devon sail through the air, splash into the water across the mouth of the flowing river . . . and a few seconds later saw me lifting it out of the water for another cast.

Then I nearly fell into the lake. For, a couple of casts later, I got a vicious strike. You can imagine the thrill of it: this lake in lower Chile with its snow-capped volcanoes; not knowing even the name of the very fish I was fishing for . . . where he was? . . . what would catch him? . . . was I merely playing the fool? and—BANG! came the confirmation that I had been right. I think fishermen who have fished strange places, experimenting both for spots and what to use, will realise my almost alarmed anxiety to get that fish in the boat.

He never jumped once, as I remember, nor was he anything like as clever as a trout or small-mouth bass—he just jerked and ran, jerked and ran. And in a few minutes I had him slapping about on the floor boards of the boat. He was as I have just described him; and so I examined him while the Indian made little gurgling sounds . . . holding up the Devon to me . . . making sign-talk equivalent to: 'What is this magical thing?'

Well . . . it wasn't magical for so very long. Without moving from the point where the Indian was holding the skiff against a rising wind, I got two more of these. The biggest was about two pounds. Then . . . a bigger one . . . yes, he must have been a beauty! . . . took my Devon away from me.

The line came in empty, broken just where the wire trace joined his nose, broken in the last place one would think it could be. And nothing else in my bag would stir another fish. They wanted just that one old veteran Devon which had been so useless before.

But the worst luck I had of the day was that the Herr President of the

Deutsche Klub had left, to go somewhere else on the lake while I was out fishing. And the next day I was to leave, climb high over the passes to where the rock-strewn river beds lay far below . . . to where, in a tall forest, you come on that red triangle sign, marked: CHILE—ARGENTINE . . . after which I would cross South America to Buenos Aires, and sail for France.

I went to Buenos Aires chiefly to find an exiled president of Chile, General Carlos Ibañez, whom I found living in two rooms in a none too wealthy street. Some weeks previously I had interviewed the then President, Don Arturo Alessandri, in his summer palace overhanging the Pacific at Viña del Mar, the Chilean Monte Carlo. It took me a week to persuade General Ibañez to let me see him, or even to let me know where he was (all communication was done by a go-between); and his first act, when I entered his two-room flat, was to open a little mahogany box and take out two passports.

'Mine and my wife's,' he said. 'I applied for leave to go back to Chile two days ago. The Chilean Consul sent them back to me. I cannot go home.' Then he nodded at the photograph on the wall, of three children. 'Mine,' he said, 'but they are in Chile—and I cannot bring them here. I am ruined.'

The irony of this scene consists of the fact that both of these presidents had exiled each other. In 1928 General Ibañez had shipped Don Arturo Alessandri over the Andes in the approved and gentlemanly South American fashion. The two made the couplet of the strange political story I wanted to write. And, as the world knows, General Ibañez did get back to Chile about two years after I talked with him, to lead a tragically unsuccessful revolution.

With my story in my notebooks, and my heart still skipping beats from too many months in the high Andes, I bought a steamship ticket for France to end half a year in South America. Even as we sailed down the muddy, vast River Plate I began to day-dream of England. In that patch on the Equator where it rains all the time (because a warm and cold current meet), and where the skyline is a forest of giant mushrooms whose tops are condensing vapour —where even the steel sides of the ship seem to wilt and become soggy as wet cardboard—I still hung over the rail and looked toward England.

My dreams centred on one desire. It would be May when I reached England. There is a spot where two cool little rivers meet down in Somerset. There was an hotel to which I had gone for years. There was a little group of locals who usually met in its tap room. And in there I would find rest again.

VIII

Fishing the West Country of England; reward

There is a spot in the West Country that is almost a sanctuary for a vanishing type of Englishman. There is not a day in the year when you may not kill something. Stag, hind, fox, otter, rabbits; pheasant, partridge, blackcock, woodcock, snipe, possibly some passing duck—salmon and trout. They all come in their seasons. These seasons overlap so that you may have three or four kinds of different sport in as many days. You may hunt the stag, and the next day be with a shotgun on the rolling green hills; on the next you may take your rod and try the last of the year's fishing. To these sporting Englishmen who live there, a day when something is not killed is a day of frustration, a day wasted.

But Captain Tantivy is not a bloodthirsty man, even if he may act as if he had been put on the earth to kill everything on it. It is not the killing which whips up the blood of this survival of the old English sporting squires. You will never understand Captain Tantivy until you see the aftermath of a hunt. The long ride home with the darkness settling around you. The final barbaric touch of splendour of a rainy, windy sunset over the empty moor. The tired hounds. The pink coat of the huntsman fast turning into just a black silhouette on ahead. This, and the thought of the warm bath, the restful drink, and the cosy fire that awaits you at the pub.

Yes, this, and the picture still in your mind of the 'Tufters' trying to cut a hind out of a herd in a deep stand of wintry beech in the morning, and then a batch of horsemen like an old sporting print coming hell for leather down a sheer slope of dead fern.

'Yagga-yagga-yagga! Hyeah-hyeah-hyeah! Toot-toototoot! . . . Ernest, if you can't read—ye can bloody well hear, can't you! Go back! Go back! Go back! She's turned . . . she's turned . . . ride like hell down the valley! Toot-toot-toot-yagga-yagga-yagga, you ——!'

It is perhaps with a deep satisfaction that you see the hind, fleeing for her life, bounding across the deep green farmlands that lie in the valley bottom, soaring over hedges as if catapulted on springs—deep, deep, deep into another woodland sanctuary. The hound music tingles in your veins. But you will be just as pleased when you get home to see mud-bespattered Captain Tantivy sigh that the hind ran them thirty miles—and then was not killed. For you will know that deep down in his heart Captain Tantivy is also not disconsolate. He has had a grand day. He has fulfilled himself.

That is the exciting side of this country I have been talking about. But it is not the one for which I go there. To me this English scene, where the dark rivers curve down from Exmoor, is the joy of the familiar and the luxury of my own solitude by its river banks.

Of the familiar, I know that I shall find in the tap room the water bailiff who has been on the Exe and Barle for over forty years. What he doesn't know about fish is hardly worth mentioning. Putting down his pipe, he will tell you of how he never eats fish . . . because . . . well, it must have been fifteen years ago . . . there was a year when the salmon came up the river with a disease in their gills, and when you took them out of the water they were all soft and spongy. 'And since then I never could bide a fish! I couldn't eat one.' He will tell you of the flies which are inevitably disappearing— killed by the oil seeping into the water from the tarred roads and motor cars. He hasn't seen a Green Dunham for years. The Red Spinner is getting rare. He wouldn't be at all surprised if, one day, the old trusty March Brown himself disappeared. Yes, Mr. X is dead . . . a pity . . . a fine gentleman, too. The year they took eighty-two salmon out of the river, Mr. X caught fifty-four of them. A grand gentleman. It's been a good salmon year, this one, too . . . which means it will be a bad trout year. And when I say to him that I have fished a river along which there just were no motor cars, he will sigh: 'Ay . . . that would be a grand place for the likes of we!'

And Hardy, the rabbit trapper? Well, he hasn't been so 'clever' this last winter; his back, you know. Then they took out all the rest of his teeth. But he'll be at the Lamb . . . or else you'll find him in the Lion.

And Hardy will produce his ferrets. We have stood on the opposite side of those thick sod hedges over many years. Bless his heart, he will bring a handful of ferrets into the Lion! Rosie was shot by a gentleman, who stuffed Rosie back into a hole—and said nothing about it—therefore he was not a gentleman. 'Spent all afternoon trying to find her, I did!' But Robin Hood is still alive. So is Fitchie. And here's a new one—Buffalo Bill. Hardy picks the three of them up and lets their pink noses touch his cheeks, as if they were kissing him. He has seventeen ferrets this year. And he *can* talk to them; for he would put Rosie into a hole and say: 'Now you run along *inside*, Rosie . . . . Father can go along *outside*.' And then you would see Rosie come out, blink at him with her pink eyes, as if asking what to do next!

That is part of the welcome familiar.

This was a long remove from the wild scrub country of southern Chile. It was totally different from the pine forests, and the thundering rivers of Norway I was going to fish that September. It was equally distant, in its character, from the streams of France I was going to fish in Haute Savoie within the next few weeks. But it held something which none of these other scenes could offer.

I think the best thing to call it is a certain quiet decency. This almost unchanging English scene, with its red and green rolling hills, holds a romance that wild rocks, and wild rivers, or snow-capped volcanoes could never give you. It has a gentleness, a rich rustic worth, and an unostentatiousness that is like the English character. An imperturbable scene which fills you with contentment.

You are lucky if the trout you catch here average three to the pound. Very lucky! When you come back to the hotel at night you will find that there are some plates by the door. Two, three, perhaps even ten trout may be lying on a plate. But they are just dinner plates. No salvers are needed. And you will put down your own monster—let's say that you have actually caught a half-pounder—with as much quiet satisfaction as you would drop down that six-pounder in southern Chile. In fact, considering the circumstances, you have done an even more wonderful thing.

Here with a little aluminum box in your pocket, or a few flies stuck in your coat lapel, you will fish all day with a cast so fine that it looks like a strand of a brunette's hair. Perhaps it is better to buy your leaders and flies from the fishing-fanatic in the little town near by. He stains his own leaders and ties his own flies and is so covered with flies stuck into his coat and hat himself that he looks like a veritable cockleburr. Here is another of the welcome familiars with whom it is as much of a delight to gossip about fish as it is with the water bailiff. More, in fact, because this person who runs the local bicycle and tackle shop, will leave his shop on the slightest excuse merely to catch a fish. He has, I believe, one or two anonymous flies with which he has experimented himself. But the ones he will probably recommend you are the small hackled blue upright—with most of its hackle snipped off; the Hare's Ear, Pheasant Tail, Greenwell's Glory, and, as the season gets

An imperturbable scene which fills you with contentment

on, the apparently irresistible Little Tup. Then it is a question of where and how you present the flies.

The gentle art of stream fishing in the West Country of England (I never could afford a rod on a big chalk stream) has a charm all of its own. Perhaps that is just why I have never tried to fish for salmon on this river, although I have certainly fished it double the number of times I have fished any loch or river in Scotland. As I have said, I enjoy the luxury of my own solitude, my own idle reflections—the inner solitude. There are times when I don't want trouble, I don't want thrills; I have come here for just a lazy contentment. Sometimes I do not want to do anything but lie in the sun. Fresh spring days, with the sun hot on the green meadows, when the shadows of the clouds seem to 'peel' off the hills; when the crows are still building their ragged nests in the leafless trees; when the weirs run white from the heavy flow that comes down from where the red deer lie among the bracken on Exmoor; when the sheep are lambing and you lie there, watching the ewes butt the tottering lamps away—the silly ones which don't know their own mothers. The time when the primroses are just about going and soon that little white flower, like a buttercup, will appear . . . growing in rafts above the beds of green water-weeds bending in the slacks of water.

I like to watch the plover, tumbling about in the sky over the red, ploughed fields; and Mr. Rat, emerging from his hole and going about his business; the silent, ceaseless flight of the swallows over some shallow stream.

But then, this is just about the time when you ought to be fishing. There is just the right amount of discoloration in the water. And you realise, as you wade, that small-river fishing is good for you. It breaks you of the long, careless cast that loch fishing, or the heavy river, has got you into. If you are on the shore of a loch you are always casting to see how far out you can get; the fish must be there. If you are in a boat you are always trying long casts in among the rocks along the shore; the fish must be there. If you are in the middle of a shallow loch you are always trying to drop your flies as far away as you can from your boat—in case it might have frightened them. Those are the habits which I, at least, have got into. You become careless about a slack line; to drop your flies lightly seems your only consideration. And you play fish too long.

But here, on a little river like this, you have to be canny. It is all a question of where you put your fly. The shorter your line—and the time you play your fish—the better. And you have to know water; the tempting deep places, which seem almost unable not to produce a fish, are usually as unprofitable as fishing in a ditch. But there is a long innocent stretch on the little Exe, for instance, where a line of great old oaks stretch their branches far out over the water. And if you can get your line in under there you are almost always rewarded with a couple of fine fish, usually in remarkably good condition. I don't know why this should be, except that these embarrassing oak branches happen to hang over a long stickle, and the water at that point must be particularly rich with good trout food. At any rate, fish taken from there are nearly always the best fish you will get from that mile or so of river. Then, on the Barle, you can work up a narrow stretch that rushes under a main bridge. And in here, if you can work your fly properly with the dense underbrush on either side of you, you will get fish twice the size you will ever take out of the more likely, broader water lower down. Those who have fished that bit of water will know the stretches I am talking about. They will also know the broad stretch where Exe and Barle meet—to run down into the Black Pool—where you will hardly ever catch a decent trout.

That's just what makes it all so infuriating, and delectable. There is a bridge far below with a fine stickle of water running away from it. By it is an inn. A very modest little inn, where you know if the sandwiches and bottle of beer in your bag have not been enough, you could always get a hunk of bread and cheese—and some more beer. You may sit there on a bench, tired from the weight of your waders, and have another pint or so before you begin the weary walk home at night; and, as I have said, if you have a half-pound fish to show, then you have caught a whopper.

I have fished this stretch of water at least three or four Easters . . . usually to repair from the dilapidations caused by too much London. I have fished it in September. And I have watched its flow when there were no fish, when I had come down to that part of the world, for a bit of rough shooting in the late autumn. This was chiefly for cock pheasants. The finest day I remember was a mixed bag of three cock pheasants, one partridge, a black-cock (shot, of all places! in the roots); and a woodcock that I shot in a swampy bottom, going down along a long line of red beeches just as the sun came down.

I have never caught a fish there worth talking about, except for the pleasure in catching it. But I know some of the rocks and ledges and stickles in those rivers as well as I know my own door-step. I love that county. I love the life it holds—the bogs, the spinneys; yes, even the almost vertical hills where you slip and slide in the snow of a wintry sunset. I love this English scene.

And I hope that no war, or no such evil thing as 'progress,' will ever change it.

IX

The fish chef of the old 'Olympic'; the passionate
fishermen of Haute Savoie

It is a hard choice to make, but I almost believe the Frenchman is a more implacable fisherman than either the English or American. We all know de Maupassant's story of the two old comrades who went to fish outside the walls during the siege of Paris, were captured by the Germans and shot as spies, after which the jeering Germans ate their fish. And on the eve of this last war, the very last week before it, in fact, I fished in a slack water behind an island below Strasbourg with an old Frenchman in his rowboat, with the French soldiers climbing up ladders to their lookouts in the trees, staring malevolently at similar German sentries across the racing Rhine. We were using maggots to catch fish none of which could be larger than a long cigar; but this innkeeper-fisherman had invested his life's savings to buy a pub in this particular spot—so that he could follow his hobby in his off-hours (they were more off than on!)—and now, he complained bitterly, the dirty Boche would one day cross the pontoon bridge and . . . he would never fish again.

'Or perhaps they will merely use a cannon and shoot me where I am!'

He would not move, however, until that day.

I do not know whether anyone else has ever witnessed it, but I have never seen one of those French fishermen catch anything but the bottom where the Seine flows through Paris. Yet think how many businesses were being neglected, how many of those useful French wives were tending shop, while these Frenchmen, by their hundreds, sat on the banks of the Seine with the scantiest hope that they could bring something home that would justify them for a wasted day. I call that courage.

If you drive down across France in the spring, when the streams are full and the leaves are their bright vivid green, you will sometimes think that half of France must be out with rod and grub or worm. You will see (at least, you did one day) the Frenchmen sitting by their poplar-lined canals. Sometimes, with a little lead minnow with a hook in its tail. You will see them leaning over the shore-end of a bridge by some fresh river, jerking their rod up and down, up and down, up and down. . . . They are fishing for yellow perch. And many a time I have got out of my car and watched these Frenchmen. I have an affinity with them—and an equal anxiety as to what they might be about to catch. I know the black-barred perch; and the spectacle of one of these Frenchmen always recalled spring days in a canoe on the windy lake back home. Ask them a pertinent question. And the Frenchman, seeing you are a knowledgable angler, responds with a discourse on local habits.

Finally you are both rewarded; he has got one! '*Eh, bien! M'sieu—demi-kilo!*' And some stocky, jovial Frenchman of the Midi, free from all inhibitions concerning the social values of fishing, will inform you that this monster he is holding up must weigh at least a pound.

I have found, on such occasions, that if you go with this Frenchman (and his trophy) to his favourite little sidewalk café in some sunbaked village square you will come nearer to his heart—what he really thinks about life and politics—than you possibly could by bribe or guile. He feels, as a fellow fisherman, that he can talk straight with you. You have the common bond. And if you happen to be on a journey in which time is of no importance he will introduce you in the evening to the members of his village fishing club. There is hardly a village in all France which does not have one.

These clubs are not altogether unknown in either England or America, but they are extremely rare. In France they are an institution. Many of them are for more than merely the local coarse fish; they exist in the trout regions where their democracy is just as unblemished. This is particularly true in Haute Savoie, where the swift green rivers race down through the pine forests and grey crags; and where, in most other countries, you would find every foot of such good water owned by some rich proprietor. I had passed in and out of Paris for years, often with weeks to spare, wondering whether it was worth the bother to find where I could buy the right to fish for trout, and then always giving it up because it seemed too complicated. Then by an off-chance I picked a tiny village high up in the mountains of Haute Savoie to settle down in and write my book on South America. And here I found the poor trout fisherman's heaven.

As I drove past Lake Annecy I stopped at the local fishing shop to see what kind of flies they were using, and get some. I was amazed at the 'elegance' of this little tackle shop, its window display, its show-cases, its long line of rods—it might have been in Pall Mall or St. James's Street. There was such a professional competence in its air. But what gave me such a start, almost a shock, was that when the proprietor turned round to speak to me from a leader he was tying I found myself looking at the twin brother of the little bicycle-and-tackle shop man I had left only a few days before back in Somerset.

Later, when we were fishing one of the mountain rivers together, I told him about this. But this day when I waited for him to straighten up I found that he couldn't; he was a hunchback. And later, on the river, he told me why he could never stand upright again; he had been 'hunchbacked' on the Somme —shot through the spine. Not only that, but when our acquaintance improved he took me to the fine little hotel he had once owned in Annecy, and had sold so that he could run just his small tackle shop. 'You may think me a fool, M'sieu, but I am a completely happy man. In the hotel I made money—but in my shop I *live!*' On the river one luncheon time, when we ate on the bouldered bank with an eagle soaring high overhead, he told me that he was a member of the Cross of Fire, the Hooded Men, the most violent Fascist organisation in all France—and that his brother had just come out from serving three months in prison, because twenty-six rifles had been found in their house.

He was the finest fly-fisher I have ever seen.

'But these flies, *M'sieu*!' he exclaimed when I went out to my car that first day and brought back my bag, 'are not the ones for here! *Pas ici!* What do you think of these?'

I told him I had never in my life seen the like of those he was showing me. He was immensely pleased. 'They are,' he said . . . half closing his eyes like some composer searching for a chord . . . 'a few experiments that I have made myself. . . . I would suggest that you try them.'

I never go into a tackle shop without coming out ruined. But on that day, because I did not know he was so genuine, I bought only three or four leaders and a dozen or so of his gnat-like experiments (whose look I did not trust at all), thanking him for mere politeness' sake. When he asked me where I was going to live in the mountains, and I told him about fifty miles up, he again closed his eyes.

'Too far, *M'sieu* . . . unless you are a goat. The river is full of gorges up there. You will never get down them. Even *I* find it almost impossible.'

I withheld my smile, staring at this satyr-like little creature before me, and listened patiently while he made me write down the names of some villages where, he told me, I should begin fishing lower down. Then with light sarcasm I asked him how could I fish those stretches of water—when I was not going to live in an hotel or an inn anywhere along that lower stretch. He replied with amazement: 'The Club!'

He then wrote down the name of a Frenchman in each of some five small villages and wished me good luck. 'Perhaps, *M'sieu*,' he said modestly, 'we might have a day on the river together?'

As this is a more or less accurate account of our conversation that impatient afternoon, for I was anxious to get on, I will merely state that I noticed the name of each Frenchman he gave me was obviously the proprietor of some inn or café (for which I thought he was pimping) and that I lost his own card, which he pressed upon me, even before I reached my own little pub, The Golden Lion.

So much for snap judgments.

A few days later I slid my car down to where the gorges ceased and entered a café. Its proprietor and a hefty daughter were serving what appeared to be the village postman, its policeman, and one or two other non-uniformed gentlemen, with some demi-litres of white wine. I asked if I could speak to the president of the village fishing club. The hairy-armed man behind the bar said that this was he. Could he do anything for me? I replied that I would like to fish this stretch of river; how much would it be? I was asked for how long? I said, possibly a couple of days—maybe more. Were there any fish here?

At that I noticed that the postman, the policeman, and the other non-uniformed gents had stopped speaking since I came in. Now I saw them staring at me intently. I was being appraised. I began to feel uncomfortable. . . .

The fat, hairy-armed man behind the bar smiled. Then he shrugged his shoulders. He said—looking at the others—'There *are* fish. . . . ' He left that statement hanging in the air; and if ever I have been told more plainly to my face, 'There are fish—providing you know how to catch them,' I don't want to be reminded of it. The others now turned from regarding me and took up their conversation again. It was a bad beginning. I paid fifteen francs a day, I think, for a week's fishing, drank a polite demi-litre of white wine, and left the hotel. It required all my courage to ask the proprietor did he mind if I left my car, for safe-keeping, before his hotel. He said no, he didn't mind. That was all.

The rivers up there are all snow-fed, many of them are glacial; so that even in mid-summer you will find long, swift stretches where it is hard to wade. Up by the Golden Lion, as the little satyr in Annecy had prophesied, there were gorges. And sides so steep that it was torture to get down to fish the few pools that lay between them. I had tried. I had slipped and slid down through the heavy pine forests (almost breaking my rod) to fish a few of these pools—but there was no way that I could find to get either down or up to fish the next pool. Nothing but a steep climb up the mountain-side, a walk along the mountain road, and then another descent to get down to fish another pool. I found it no good. Not for me. Although the proprietor of the Golden Lion (that excruciating man) did exclaim when I brought home a few fish from my first attempt: 'There! You see I was not lying when I wrote to you that my hotel had kilometres of fine trout fishing!'

But down here was the beginning of orchard country, and alpine wheat. The river was broad, with long beds of grey boulders that now lay bare in the sun. There were farms on one side and slopes of steep pine forest on the other, and grey iron-streaked cliffs. An inspiring country. As I put my rod together and soaked the leader I saw long stickles and channels of water coursing

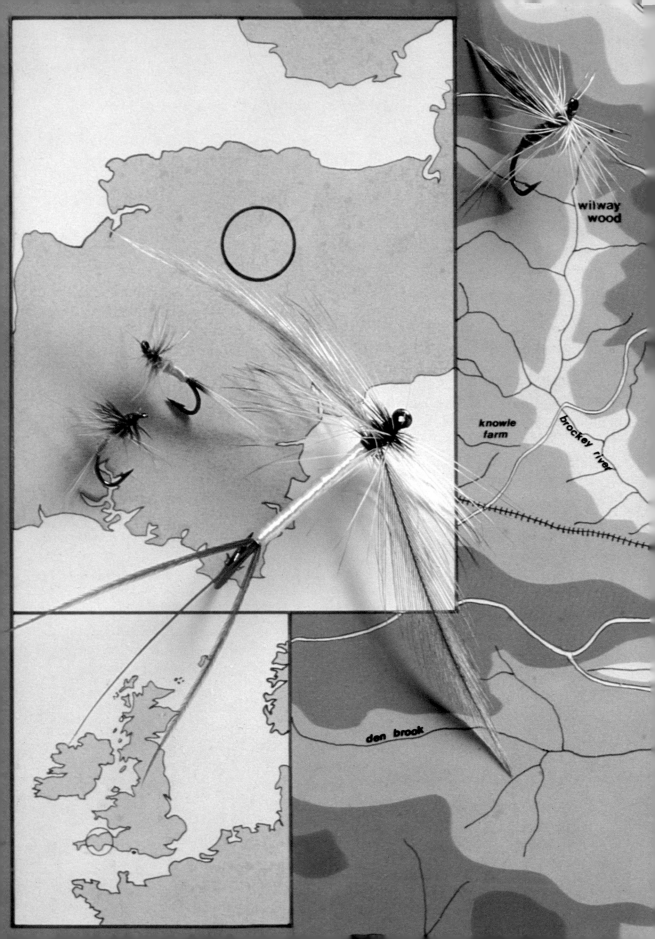

wilway
wood

knowle
farm

brockey river

den brook

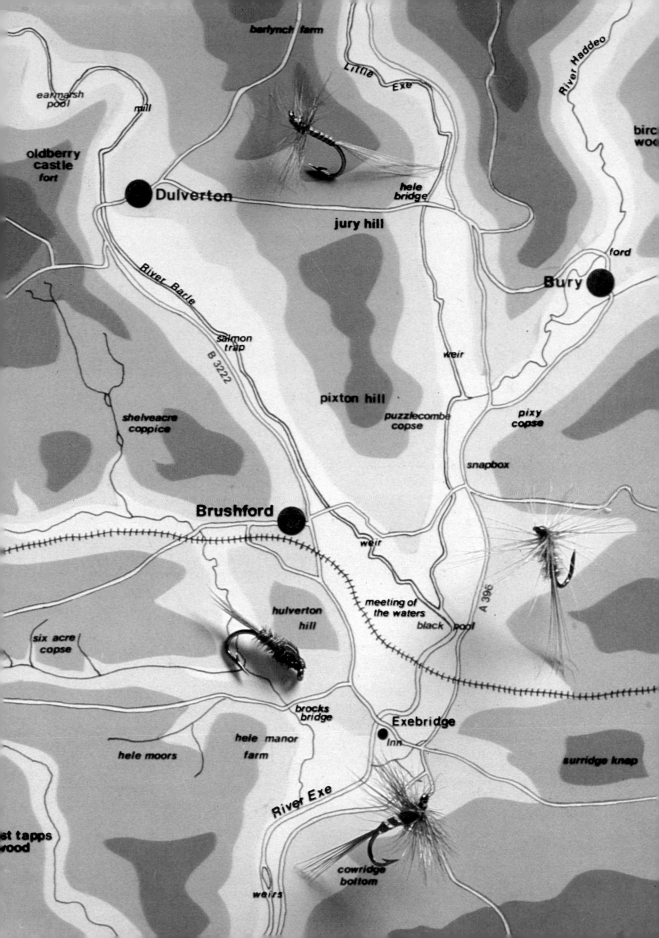

between the islands made by boulders bared by the falling water. There were long broad sweeps where the river was apple-green. And, very wisely, I put on the satyr's leader.

These were light-backed trout with vivid red spots, which struck (when they did strike) with a vicious intensity. This river was not a glacial one, and in that ice-clear water I could watch a large part of their fight. In one deep stretch of river, where it was so flat and slow that it was almost like a shallow lake, I got the best fish of the afternoon by putting on an old worn Mayfly. It was a freak attempt, but continuous rises under the branches of some trees on the far side of the pool tempted me. It was about all I could do, wading out till the water seeped over into my waders (and how cold it was!), to get my fly across to them. Time and again I watched it float, unnoticed, down under the branches; then there was a quick splash. I walked backward up on to the island of boulders again. After an exciting few minutes' fight I netted a fine little fish that was over $1\frac{1}{2}$ lb.

But although I can say I have scarcely ever seen such fine trout water, I did not touch many trout. The reason explained itself about 5 o'clock, when I saw a man emerge from the bushes opposite me (I had crossed the river to the opposite side from the village) and fix a wood grub to a reel-less line that was wrapped around an ordinary bamboo rod. He pitched this grub in and let it drift down to a pool that I had been casting over, which began under a leaning tree. Dumbfounded—I recognised him as one of the non-uniformed gentlemen I had seen at mid-day sitting in the inn—dumbfounded, I say, and a little angry, I saw him pull out a nice nine- or ten-inch trout.

Such competition was too formidable. I watched Frenchman after Frenchman appear, fix on a grub (I learned they got them from Geneva) and pop it into the water. It seemed as if the whole village was down by 6 o'clock, including the postman. I gave it up. I had eight fish, none of which was up to half a pound, except the one lucky one; yet I felt I could now walk with impunity back to that village inn. And there, tired, I sat down at a table before its arboured door and ordered a litre of white wine.

The hefty daughter came out to serve me, smiling now. '*Et vous? M'sieu—bonne chance?*'

I pulled aside the grass inside my bag and showed her the big one. The next person who came out was the proprietor: '*Bien?*' he asked.

Light-backed trout with vivid red spots

I repeated my performance—with the one big fish. He did not say any-thing. But, as I had not taken my rod apart—it was leaning against the car—he walked over, and picked it up. He tried it with his wrist. Then (and I watched him do that so carefully) I saw him looking at the flies. He nodded. Then he came back and sat down at the table beside me, tapping it idly with his fingers.

'Where did you get that one?' he asked, meaning my one big fish.

So that's the way it began. I was there a couple of months that summer, writing my book; and every afternoon I fished the streams or rivers around me. I have seldom found more congenial, pithy companions than these Frenchmen of the village fishing clubs. The presidency of the club, I learned, was an honour which was supposed to rotate yearly. The proprietors of the village inns or cafés always took it in turn—because it brought such cus-tomers! The return from the river always led direct to the café, where the day's luck was discussed. For this it was necessary to have a demi-litre, per-haps several demi-litres of white wine. They were not all grub fishermen. An occasional elderly man (perhaps the village doctor) would amble back with a fly rod, and make some acid remarks about the rest of the company.

But they all loved fishing. They loved talking about fishing even more, perhaps; but they loved just fishing itself so much that it was not long before I discovered that any stretch of river within an easy walk of one of these villages was simply fished to death. Talk about 'too many rods on the water'; their bamboo poles looked almost like a fence at times.

And so, as his name was like a legend along the river, I called up the little hunchback down in Annecy. Should we, I asked, have a day's fishing on the river together? He asked me to wait a moment. He always called his chubby red-haired little wife '*Mon petit*' (as fat Sacha Guitry used to call his beloved Yvonne Printemps); and I could hear him cajoling her now—the discussion obviously being, would she look after the store? Then his bright voice came back to me:

'Of a certainty! Tomorrow, 9 o'clock precisely, I shall meet you at—'

He was at loss for a name, for, he said, 'there is no village there.' But he gave me a rendezvous about fifteen miles below where I had been fishing all the time! 'I shall wait for you by the road,' came his eager injunction; 'I have a little red Citroën coupé—stop when you see it!'

By now I had reached that place in the confidence of M. Vacheron, proprietor of the *Lion d'Or*, to know that he had been the 'fish chef' on the old *Olympic*. He had cooked in the 'private' restaurant, that *de luxe* dining-room, where millionaires and movie stars gorged themselves across the Atlantic. They had seventeen chefs for, on the average, only thirty-eight people. He was a distinguished man.

'Mr. Pierpont Morgan,' said M. Vacheron, '*always* ordered oysters *au gratin* and lobster Newberg.'

This night, learning that I was to fish with the celebrated M. Croisier, he wondered if it might not be possible for me to bring some of my trout back alive—as some of the Frenchmen did in these parts with a little barrel or tin can of water on their backs. I firmly told him no; we would have to continue in our usual way. I did not intend to burden myself in these rough streams with any additional pounds of wobbling water.

'Very well,' sighed M. Vacheron; 'I would like to cook you the true *truite au bleu*. But for that I must have them alive. I cook them alive and then clean them afterwards. If you cannot bring them back alive, then you must mark the two or three you have caught last—the last to die—and I shall do with these. These I shall cook. The colour will not be *truite au bleu*—but they will taste almost as good.'

M. Vacheron lived over his past, with the aid of many cognacs, every night, and now, dejected because of my refusal to provide him with live trout, he declared: 'The golden age of cooking is over, M. Farson. It is the sauces. Truffles and cream and butter—even the big restaurants aren't so free with these any more. From our point of view (the chefs') probably the finest restaurant in the world was the old Café Royal in London when Mrs. Nobel owned it. . . . Ah . . . everything! . . . hundreds of truffles . . . all the butter you wanted . . . if a dish was not precisely correct . . . you threw it in the fire. . . .'

'And some of the dishes we used to prepare. . . . The *Crêpes Veux-tu?* . . . ! They were pancakes cooked in apricot brandy . . . with lizards done on them in meringue . . . with cherry eyes . . . and then little piles of fresh peaches and pineapple piled up all around . . . !'

As we sat in his kitchen, where he held these nightly reminiscences, the rain ran in rivers down its window panes. There had been a cloud-burst that day. And we had seen a staggering thing—a farmhouse up on the alpine meadow behind us struck by lightning. It was one of those Swiss-chalet affairs, with broad stones holding down the shingles of its roof. It went up in one grand blaze as if a high explosive had hit it. We had watched it from our balcony.

Its owners were away, having just taken their cattle to graze on a higher alpine slope. 'And now,' said the sophisticated M. Vacheron, 'they have lost all their money—it is burning there now—for, M. Farson, you know a French peasant never puts his money in a bank. He doesn't trust banks.'

I, selfishly, was only worried about this rain; would it spoil my day tomorrow with M. Croisier? I awoke early to a clear blue sky over the glisten-ing pine forest, drank my bowl of coffee, leapt into the car—and swerved and slithered down the slippery mountain road to where I found a little red Citroën almost lying on its side in a ditch in a deep forest twenty-five miles below. M. Croisier was in an exultant mood: 'We shall have a fine day!'

The only habitation we passed that day was a saw-mill. For mile after mile the river sides here were too steep for farming. That is why there were no villages. That is why there were so many trout. But M. Croisier fished in a peculiar way; he fished with a wet fly, up-stream, throwing the fly *directly* ahead of him. He got thirty-seven trout and I got, I think, seventeen.

But what fishing!

We cast with lines not much longer than our rods. We fished behind every rock, boulder, ledge. And M. Croisier even took fish from dead against the bank. Tap-Tap-Tap went M. Croisier.

'But!' I protested at first, 'you don't leave your flies on the water long enough for any fish to touch them!'

The little hunchbacked man smiled: 'Do not worry, M. Farson. If the trout are there—I shall get them.'

The point was, he explained, that where the stream was so swift, and especially after this cloud-burst in the upper mountains, the trout just *couldn't* leave any lee they had found—that was why, he said, we would find so many of them right up against the bank. And again, if we let our lines rest on the water for more than an instant, we would have our leaders swept back against our own waders. 'No!—it must be like that!'—and he put his flies behind a rock before us just as if they were on the end of a wand.

I have never seen anything like it.

Nor have I ever seen anything like his eagerness. There were one or two fairly large pools or riffles that we approached. But before I could get up to them the little satyr raced on ahead of me. He couldn't resist it. *'Pardon, M'sieu!'* he always said, apologising for his selfishness—then raced me to the next pool just the same. The forest, rocks, glistening racing water, were all so fresh that sun-filled morning, with the white clouds scudding across the blue sky overhead, that I felt too full of the sheer joy of living to mind much what he did—but, I decided, the next time M. Croisier and I went out *I* would put on running shoes.

There was a pool by the saw-mill, with some logs in it which were waiting to be cut. Here M. Croisier put his fly rod down and took a short little rod, about the size of a section of trout rod, from his back. It was a stout little piece, with an off-cast wire loop at its tip. This, said the satyr, was a 'Dandinet.' He then took from his bag a wooden spreader very similar to those you see in tackle-shops around which are wound hand-lines for sale. But on this one was nothing but yards and yards of stout gut—just, let us say, some sixty or a hundred yards of a leader. And on the end of this M. Croisier slid a little lead minnow—after which he attached a hook to the end of the gut.

'You see,' he said, giving it a flick, 'I can cast this anywhere.'

The little lead minnow shot through the air . . . the gut unwound off the spreader as easily as a thread-line off a Silex reel, and *plunk!* the minnow fell into the pool, say, about forty yards from us. The instant it hit the water M. Croisier was already winding it in with swift revolutions of the wooden spreader. And this he did with the speed with which you would bring back your Devon with a bait-casting reel.

A fish took the minnow. When it jumped I saw the lead minnow shoot yards up the gut-line. 'You see,' exulted the expert M. Croisier, 'when the minnow shoots up the line they have nothing to shake against. . . .'

It was purely for my amusement, he said, that he had brought the 'Dandinet' along. And then to show me what he really could do with it, he shot the minnow up-stream where the river entered the pool. And again he retrieved it. 'But this, M. Farson . . . is not like fly-fishing!'

I still had a lot of my two months to go, and this was the beginning of a friendship M. Croisier told me that—and very plainly.

The way it came about was that at the end of the day, before we began the long walk back to our cars, for we had been fishing up-river all this time, we reached a village. Here, after a stiff climb up the river bank, M. Croisier and I rested ourselves in its small inn's yard. We had a few litres of white wine. And during this I attempted to pay him for some leaders and flies I had borrowed from him on the river. He held up his little hand in dismay:

'M. Farson! No! In my little shop in Annecy, I shall charge you for *everything—beaucoup!* But on the river, M. Farson . . . on the river we are comrades!'

It was a gesture from *la belle France* I shall never forget.

X

The swift rivers of Norway

If, on some high Norwegian tableland, you have ever felt the crisp reindeer moss crunch beneath your boots (and it is possible to shoot wild reindeer less than a hundred miles outside Bergen); if you have ever sat and stared down, tracing the green fingers of the Atlantic as they feel their way into the rocky, fissured fjords—knowing that a river you hope to fish, almost directly opposite you, will take a day and a night and another day to reach by car and boat, whereas that trusty, overworked old crow could get there easily in two hours—if you have ever stood thigh-deep and felt the 'pull' of those great rivers, thundering hundreds of miles through the pine forests on their way to the sea, then . . .

I leave it to anyone who has fished in Norway to put the end to that sentence. I can't. I fish for words, and the terms 'primitive' and 'majestic' come to me automatically; but there is something starkly stupendous about Norwegian fishing to which these words do not measure up. We will leave it at that.

In Oslo, at lunch with the president of the Sports Club and Lairdahl Grieg, we decided that most of the good fishing in Norway had either been rented or bought outright by rich foreigners, mostly Englishmen; that to take a rod on one of the poorer rivers was very largely a waste of time; and that the whole thing, to fish that way, was too much of a commercial proposition, anyway. Better try prospecting in some of the remote, more inaccessible parts. This was agreed.

'I know a place,' said the president of the Sports Club. 'It's up in the heart of the country—forty miles from the nearest decent road. That is remote enough—as your poor car will tell you. It's called Gjendesheim.'

He had not exaggerated. A few days later I left the main road in central Norway and struck westwards along what could be classed as nothing more than forty miles of ruts and bumps through a deep pine forest, to come out at sunset on one of a series of step-like lakes set in terrific mountains. Here there was an excellent hotel—with nothing but Norwegians in it—and I rented a log cabin by the shore of a river which tumbled down from this lake to the one below. At nights we slept in board bunks with a big fire of pine-knots burning on the open-hearth fire. Reading the galley-proofs of the South American book I had finished in Haute Savoie, I fished there several weeks.

To wake up in a room lined with nothing but smooth, scented, unpainted pine planks; wash in that crisp, cold Norwegian air; then eat a breakfast of fresh 2-lb. trout, jugs of milk, slabs of butter and crisp bread—or pickled herring, meat balls, smoked salmon, salad, or what will you—that is one of the 'husky' factors of this Norwegian fishing which makes the experience so baffling to all adjectives. You feel alive as you have never felt before!

The river itself was less than fifteen yards from my cabin door. I had fallen asleep listening to its roar. I might say there was one of the inevitable Englishmen there—a recluse who owned a log cabin, with a sod roof, on the opposite bank of the river from mine. He warned me: 'Do not go out in it without a stout pole. I never do. You can easily get swept off your feet and end up in the Atlantic Ocean.' As he was going climbing that first day he loaned me his own wading pole, until I could find one; and his had a stout steel tip.

As I have said repeatedly, you will find no record, nor even grand-sized fish in this book; the largest fish I caught at Gjendesheim weighed less than three pounds. But then, the rest were always between one and two pounds; and they were all caught in this swift water. The one which weighed less than three pounds did not, on the other hand, weigh so very much over two.

The particular fascination of this fishing lay in trying to reach the most inaccessible parts of the river, which were of course the parts least fished. It was almost like a game. Then, too, another thing that had to be guarded against was that you might step off the comparatively safe perch of one rock—and go down over your neck. The bottom of the river was as broken as the Alps. So of course I had my worst experience my first day, as fools do.

I had taken one or two fish of over a pound each from a fast strip of comparatively smooth water out beyond where the river frothed through a rip of rocks. It had been an exciting battle to get them because it was inevitable that my line should foul some rocks before I could work the fish into the water directly below me. I was feeling rather pleased with myself. Particularly as I had noticed two or three Norwegians sunning themselves on the bank, idly watching me. I edged a little farther out, wedged the Englishman's stout pole firmly between two rocks, and began paying out line as deftly as I could to make a long cast and shoot the line out into the middle of that tempting bit. And there I got a two-pound trout on the first cast.

Not only that, the downward sweep of the trout carried my line safely past the rocks which had previously fouled me, and I had him in the water below me without much fuss. I knew I daren't try to hold him and work down to him—so I began to pull this fighting two-pound fish up against the stiff current. He was so far below me that I knew I could not get his head out—I have done this, taken a chance, and scuttered a fish up against a swift stream—so I just held him at stages, hoping he would get tired. I did not doubt my tackle, for I began Norway with entirely fresh leaders; nor did I doubt that he was firmly hooked. It was merely a question of patience—and I was rewarded.

By this time, out of the tail of my eye, I noticed that the Norwegians on the bank were all standing up. They were almost as interested as I was. So it was with a certain degree of pride that I slipped my net under this two-pound beauty. In fact, I turned slightly to watch the Norwegians (for their approval) as I lifted him out of the water. Then the trout fell through a hole in my wretched net. . . .

That net was the one thing which wasn't fresh when I began in Norway. I had patched it too much in France. Now I was to pay for it.

In my excitement I took my arm from around the supporting pole, stepped forward, as if to catch the fish with my hands, and stepped into a pocket between the boulders. Fish, net, and I started off on our hundred-mile journey to the Atlantic. At that moment I realised I had £100 in Travellers' Cheques in my pocket, just given me by my publisher Lairdahl Grieg down in Oslo as an advance payment on my South American book. *This water would cancel my signatures!* I then fetched up with a bang against another projecting rock, saw that I could stand up, and saw that I still had the fish on.

I think those Norwegians must have thought I was mad. For I played the fish—with my line through my net—and he was so dead beat by now that I practically wrapped it around him. Then I staggered to the bank. The Norwegians, who had come down to save me, saw a man running back and forth along the bank . . . putting bits of paper under small stones! Whether they thought it was some sacred rite, I do not know; they did not come near me. Then, as the cheques dried, I lay on my back and put my legs up into the air to get the water out of my waders. I finally found the fish flapping about on the grass, with the hook stuck in the twisted net. It had almost got back into the river again.

But the fishing was not up to what I had been promised it would be. And one morning when I had decided to get up and fish at dawn—I saw the reason why. I saw two shock-headed Norwegian peasants coming back from the very stretch of water I had intended to fish—*with 100 yards of net!* Now I knew why we had pound- and two-pound trout for every breakfast, when the few of us fishing could not possibly have caught that many. I also knew why we could not have caught that many. And I knew why we had to drown ourselves, almost, trying to reach inaccessible spots in the river in order to touch a big fish. I was furious.

Two lakes high up in the mountains that I had been told were stiff with trout I had never got a rise on. When I had come down at sunset a few nights back, tired, bewildered, from the highest lake, a Norwegian diplomat staying at the little hotel by my log cabin had laughed at me.

'But there are no trout there. Ab-solutely none! The peasants netted both those lakes last autumn.'

'Why?'

'Because they had been told there would be a good market for smoked trout.'

'But why don't you *stop* them?'

'We can't. In Norway the local farmers own the fishing rights of the

Then the trout fell through a hole in my wretched net. . . .

water, and of the rivers and streams that run through their property. They can do what they like—up to a certain point.'

That point, he explained, was if a farmer wanted to *sell* his river rights. He could rent them to whomever he wanted, but when it came to selling them to some outsider—then the Community must have its say.

'If the Community likes the outsider,' he said, quite unconscious of how strange it all sounded, 'then it is all right. If they think he is a scamp—then he may not buy the fishing rights. In any case, the Community must give its permission.'

The Community is made up of the local farmers.

It was not the new Labour government, insisted the diplomat, but half a century of tradition, which was responsible for the laws which maintain and preserve the independence of the small Norwegian farmer. Water-power companies used to buy river rights for a paltry sum from the unsuspecting farmer—then they turned his water-fall into a power station: now the law has it that before a sale is made the Community must be consulted, and in addition to the flat sum paid down, the water-power company must pay a yearly sum to the peasant. If a peasant sells his farm now it is usually obligatory for the buyer, in addition to the initial sum, to pay him a certain sum yearly.

'You know what farmers are,' said this diplomat. 'In the old days, when they'd sold their farm they came into Oslo or Bergen, lived high for a time, and then either drank it all up or squandered it. They were not used to such a big sum of money. So we think it better now to protect them from themselves.'

'Yes, but these fishing rights!' I insisted. 'Can't you make them see that they are cutting off their own noses by exercising their netting rights? They could buy more fish with the rental money than they net!'

'Ah—but that would not be independence.'

Whatever their slogan, I pointed out testily, the Norwegian peasantry, by netting their rivers, were killing the most profitable goose that ever laid a golden egg—the sporting Englishman.

This particular morning, when I had seen the 100 yards of net, I did not fish. Instead I took my rods apart and put them in their cases. And at breakfast I again tackled the diplomat.

'Your explanation,' I told him, 'sounded to me the other day like very fine applied socialism. But, tell me, did you come up here to Gjendesheim to fish this river?'

He said that of course he had.

Then I told him about the 100 yards of net I had seen that dawn. It shook him a bit, but it did not defeat him. He said they were only exercising their rights, this Norwegian peasantry: their complete independence.

'Well,' I said unhappily, 'there is probably no race on earth that I love more than the Norwegians. But I have had about all the independence I can bear in this place. I'm leaving.'

The road was tortuous, as I indicated at the beginning of this chapter; but a few days later I was driving along one of the longest glaciers in the world to get down into the fjord of Olden. Here, I had heard, I could get some sea-trout fishing. And there, I found, the fishing had been bought up. I told the man sadly, at the hotel, that I would be leaving. Then I went in to eat my dinner.

While I was doing it a fine, grey-haired old man walked in. He made that short, little ceremonial bow that the Norwegians give you; then he said— Did you write *Over Alle Grenser?*'

I bowed, and said that I had.

He held out his hand. 'There is room enough on the river for all three of us,' he said. 'My son is here, come and meet him.'

Owing to the present unhappy circumstances of splendid Norway I shall not give his name. But he was a distinguished figure in Norwegian life. Not only that, he and his tall son were two of the finest fishermen it has ever been my good luck to meet. They made the long, sweeping Norwegian cast, with which, it seems, you can keep any length of line that you want to in the air —then shoot it across the broadest river. It was something entirely new to me, and I spent days practising it.

The day before I arrived there they had caught ten fish, three of them over eight pounds. As it would happen, there were heavy storms in the mountains behind us the night I met this fine man, so that when we woke up in the morning the river was in a clouded whirling spate.

I fished there a few days with them, getting one 4½-pounder, which, with only my little Duplex, was about all I could handle anyway. The father got a 5-pounder. We toasted ourselves in *aqua-vitæ*, with which they sang little Norwegian drinking-songs, while we warmed ourselves before a fire of pine-logs and discussed what we might have done better that day. The old man had been out in a skiff for part of it, worked slantwise against the current by two men on shore, with long ropes.

Then I said goodbye and began the long, tortuous drive back into Germany.

There is a sad sequel to this story. Ten days after this war began, when I was passing through Norway, I went considerably out of my way to shake this fine old Norwegian by the hand. He was at the bottom level of despair. Half-heartedly, he showed me some photographs of his fishing the previous summer; one of a day when he and his son had caught five sea trout of over ten pounds each. But he put the pictures away with a distasteful gesture.

'I shall not fish again until the war is over,' he said bitterly. 'It would be shameful . . . when there is so much misery.'

XI

Yugoslavia; mountain climbing; and poaching the Regent's river

In that mountainous corner where Austria, Italy, and Yugoslavia meet, the Yugoslavs were quietly making a sportsman's paradise. This was chiefly because of the ski-huts they were building in the Dinaric Alps. Even in mid-summer you could climb along snow-faces for days. You could lose yourself in the snow-fog, as I have done, feel that this time, for a certainty, your number was up—then have a break in the mist and see three chamois staring at you from a landmark of red rocks. From these snows come streams, then rivers, which hold some of the finest trout in all Europe. And while it may seem a strange statement, the finest consistent trout fishing I have ever had was in the mountains of Slovenia.

To illustrate what I mean by consistent I will say that one dusk I took twelve trout out of the Savitca, every one of them over a pound, of which the largest weighed a kilo. The next night I took eleven, all over a pound. The next night I took ten, all over a pound. The number dwindles because I was fishing a restricted spot; I was poaching the Regent's river. This will be no news to him, because he found that out, and refused to give me an interview as a consequence. What he doesn't know is that, after he had come up to his little hunting-lodge in the mountains, and discovered me, I still poached his river at nights at least once a week.

Whether he or I shall ever see that river again is a thing that interests me greatly.

These rivers came down from a tableland of tumbled mountains many of whose northern faces were covered with perpetual snow. You could climb with the spring in that part of the world, for when the snows melted away in the lower clearings and the first crocus pushed up through unmelted snow pockets, the forest was still dark winter. When the beech leaves were glinting along the lake shore their buds were still closed tight a few thousand feet higher up. The banks of the lower streams became blue with gentians; the big, bell-like gentian and the little one of the brighter hue. The alpine valleys became a carpet of wildflowers, and soon, as you climbed, you came on primulas, pink, mauve, and yellow among the higher rocks. Then a climb to reach an edelweiss became a breathless risk.

In these mountains, where a man had been killed, the peasants painted and put up a little memorial ikon to a rock or tree. If Hans was painted upside down, you knew he had fallen from a cliff. If he was painted lying prone on the ground, with another man standing with an axe or a saw in his hand, then you knew a tree had fallen upon him while they were logging. They were painted with a primitive earnest skill. So were the peasant paintings of the Saints on the white walls of all the little churches. St. Christopher was the favourite, shown carrying Christ across the water on his shoulder. The three inns upon the lake were owned by a Holy Order. Mine was called the St. James. Next to it was a little church called the Holy Ghost. And here at a certain Sunday every spring the peasants came to hold a service for the May-fly.

I never knew the reason. But for two years I watched them gather there, all of them carrying umbrellas, all praying on the Day of the Mayfly.

It was a pastoral land, where the valley filled with the tinkle of cow and goat and sheep bells at sunset . . . as the boys brought them down. Then, one night, you heard the rattle of carts going by; the peasants were taking all their cattle up into the higher alpine meadows.

Up there there were seven lakes; one pink, one aquamarine blue, one royal blue, one green. And in the wilderness of rocks that lay around them there was another memorial, not quite so sympathetic. It was to three Russian soldiers who had escaped from the Germans. They lay in the grave which they had been made to dig before the Germans shot them. The Yugo-slav Alpine Club had put up a plaque to them. You could climb Triglav, and look down into Italy. And in these high passes I have seen Slovenians climb back, escaping from Mussolini, that sawdust Caesar.

There were wild strawberries on the sunny slopes.

I have never seen such beautiful trout. In the swift, icy, bouldered Savitca their backs were a pale mauve. Their spots were vivid scarlet. In the lake itself I once caught one trout, weighing over a kilo, which was darker but which must have had a million scarlet spots. He was so beautiful that I wanted to put him back. But he had almost killed himself before he would let me take him. Then there was a golden grayling, which, with its deep sides, rose sharply in the swift runs and almost broke your line before he would let you land him. This *esche* was much more prized in the Balkans than any trout. With his small mouth you would not think him capable of such a fight.

The swift Savitca splayed out into the lake over a shelf of round rocks. It swung against the far bank in its last rush. Standing on the bouldered other side you cast into the swift stream pouring down the far bank. When a fish struck he almost pulled your arm down. He was like a fighter who leaps from his chair and fights from the tap of the gong. In such water there is no time for either fish or man to sulk. In the early spring they are in the river. When the water loses its pace a bit they move out into the lake. Then, when the lake warms, they move up into the river again. But now, in the hot July suns, the snows are melting furiously in the upper mountains; the Savitca is liquid ice. And you dare not fish it without waders—or else your legs will swell.

The *Fischer* had told me that there were 10-pound trout in this lake. I had never believed him. Then one day when I was wading out to cast over the edge of this bouldered shelf a great black shape shot past me. It was after a trout of at least a kilo. The trout took refuge under the branches of a tree that had caught, swept down, upon the pebbled tableland. I watched the drama. I could almost see the little trout gasping for breath; it had been so frightened. The big cannibal trout lay at the door of the tree, waiting for it. As slowly as I could I removed my leader and tried to put a little Devon on

141

my line. It might break my rod, but it would have been worth it. Flash—the long, black, cannibal trout had seen my movement—and he was gone.

This *Fischer* was the curse of this mountain paradise. He—and the Authority; a fox-terrier little bureaucrat, wearing a green hat with an enormous chamois brush.

'You must pay 150 dinars State tax,' said the Authority.

That is about 15 shillings, not much more than a trout licence in Somerset, but—

'You must pay 10 dinars every day that you fish.'

'To whom?'

'To the State.'

Well, a shilling a day was not much, but—

'You must give up all the trout. You may buy them back for 45 dinars a kilo.'

'From whom?'

'From the State.'

'But they are my trout.'

'They belong to the State. All the trout belong to the State. If you do not want to buy them the State will not charge you for them. The State will keep them.'

'Well, what next?'

'You must have a "*Fischer.*"'

'Oh, come now!' I remonstrated. 'Surely, you don't mean that I have to take a man with me when I wade up these streams?'

The Authority nodded.

Unofficially, he was a charming person. I liked his little green hunting-suit, and the metal edelweiss attached to the stern of his green *Jäger* hat.

'But I'm not a spy!' I protested. 'Surely, I do not have to be watched all the time?'

'It is an Ordinance,' said the Authority.

I attempted to defy it. The first day, I went off in a boat by myself on the lake. I rowed to a remote elbow of it. I rose a 1½-lb. trout. And I lost it.

'*Schade!*' came a voice from the bushes on the bank. 'What a pity!'

A man stood there eyeing me. He was not dressed in that soft Jäger green, yet I knew that his brown velvet suit was an official uniform of some sort. He did not wear a chamois brush, nor did he carry a shot-gun on a sling.

'I,' he said, 'am the *Fischer*.'

A man stood there eyeing me

'How do you do?' I said.

'*Grüss* Gott,' he smiled benignly.

'You must,' he announced, 'have a *Fischer*.'

I now saw that on his back, instead of a rifle or a shotgun, was slung a little green barrel. It was like a monstrous green cigar with both ends clipped. I also saw that, argue as I might, I must have a *Fischer*.

I put on my waders and we went up a stream. It is much easier to write that than it is to do it, for the *Fischer* made me climb a mountain first. Then we dropped down through the pines into a gorge of grey rock, with a mountain stream racing through it. There were deep bottle-green pools, but most of the stream was waterfall, rapids, or long slides down the steep shelves of rock.

These the *Fischer* approached in a crouching position, stalking carefully among the beds of blue gentians and anemones. '*Da!*' His finger pointed to some swirls of air-clear water. Lying behind a rock I saw a trout. Its back was so light in colour that it seemed almost transparent. Again and again I tried, until the fly finally landed just above the rock, sucked round it in the eddy, and the trout took it.

He was about three-quarters of a pound, apple-green, dappled with scarlet little spots. The *Fischer* took him carefully, opened the trap door and slid him into the attenuated barrel.

That night when we came down from the mountain I had six of these beauties, splashing about in the little green barrel. Another day I got sixteen, three of which were well over a pound each. One day I got only three; but they were all over a pound and one was over a kilo. All these fish were taken back to the hotel where the *Fischer* put them into a little stream-fed pool, where they swam about happily until they were taken out and eaten.

This was all very well. I loved this contented country where I watched the crops grow and ripen, and then saw the wheat harvested with only sickles or scythes. Where, as I occasionally walked across to one particular corner of the lake I watched the villagers twisting their own ropes out of a particular kind of grass they grew for it, where the cobbler made all their shoes, and the women spun and wove, and where the upper loft of each house was a storehouse for its crops, whilst a good half of its lower floor was the stable. Its fire-house, housing its little token fire-fighting pump, had the statue of what appeared to be a Roman centurion on its wooden bell tower, pouring a bucket of water over a symbolic blaze. These people were about as self-contained as any community I had met.

And that was the way I wanted to be; I did not want that *Fischer* always at my elbow. The chief obstacle against illicit fishing was that, even if I did catch them without him, I could not bring them back to the hotel. For there I would be caught. The obvious answer to this was to cook them myself, out in the woods. And this my wife and I and my boy did for many and many a day that first summer. We did it so well—I might add in anticipation—that when we came down there the next spring, and I, smiling, shook hands with the little Authority again, he threw up his hands and said, in effect, that once I had paid him the initial 150 dinars State tax—I could do damn well what I liked. I was too much trouble.

We bought a cheap frying-pan at a town about thirty miles down below. Then, with this in my rucksack (and a pound of butter), my wife, my boy, and I set off on an apparently innocent row up the lake. The *Fischer* was always hanging around somewhere at first, watching me to see if I took out a rod. I could not conceal a trout rod; but it was easy to stick the little four-piece Bristol bait-casting rod up the sleeve of my old tweed coat. So that my first law-breaking was done with Devons. The Devon with the little red bead at its tail was a horrible killer when cast off the mouth of the Savitca. Usually, it only needed half an hour to get us four or five one- or two-pound trout. Then we would row down the lake to a long rocky peninsula, build a fire, and fry the trout, cut up into chunks, in sizzling butter.

I looked up once to find the *Fischer* standing over my shoulder when I had a frying-pan full of them. '*Nu! Nu! Nu! Herr* Farson!' was his admonition. And he shook his finger at me, wagging his head. The next morning the Authority drove up in his pony-trap, quite prepared to be nasty about things. But he had a beautiful little German weapon hung on a strap over his shoulder; a sixteen-bore shotgun, with a small-calibre rifle beneath its web—and I was so enchanted about this that he forgave me for everything. Over a couple of litres of the resin-like white wine that was grown somewhere in that region he extolled the virtues of his sporting gun: 'You see—I am equipped for either birds or deer . . . or perhaps . . . who knows? . . . it might be a chamois.'

'But of course!' I said; 'why not?' Why not a chamois?

So I broke the gun and peered through its beautifully kept barrels, admired the clean rifling, threw it up to my shoulder. And the Authority suggested we might have another litre, and clapped his hands. While the *Fischer* stood by, near the kitchen, gnashing his teeth like the wolf in Red Riding Hood.

Then the *Fischer* came down on us one night when an Austrian Count, his Countess, my wife, my boy, and I were having a glorious picnic on a rock—with the flames of our fire lighting up the boughs of the pine trees behind us—and pounced on a man whom he took to be me, but who was, to the dismay of the *Fischer*, a Captain of the Imperial Guards in Belgrade, Prince Paul's principal A.D.C. He was fishing with a piece of cheese.

I then tried, although it was not very successful, taking out just a couple of leaders and a small length of line in my pocket—and snatching out trout from the pools of a mountain stream high up behind the village. I would just cut a thin sapling and fish with that. In the still upper pools, lying on my stomach, I would let a dry fly land lightly. Or I would let a wet fly drip with the swift water behind the lee of some rock. I found it fascinating. I always felt that, this way, I would catch the fish of all fish some day; for I saw some enormous big trout lying at the bottom of these lonely pools. But, it seemed, only the little fools would take. Still, enough of them would fill the frying-pan.

There were only certain occasions when the *Fischer* ever showed any real admiration, even love, for me. These were when I caught a grayling. I got my first one below an old weir, where the full force of the water poured over, crashed against an opposite wall of rock, then shunted off into a rapid. I was fishing in the froth of bubbles and foam, so that when the grayling took my fly—it was a very worn little Blue Upright—I did not know what I had got.

But, without even seeing it the *Fischer* knew. '*Esche! Esche! Esche!*' he kept shouting, jumping up and down behind me on the bank.

Now my German is limited, so the *Fischer* and I always talked a peculiarly bastard lingo which was about one-third German and two-thirds Russian. For this part of the world had belonged to Austria before the last war; the *Fischer* had been a soldier in the Austrian army; and, so as many Austrians did, he had spent three years in a Russian prison camp in Siberia. So that when we brought that grayling home, I trying to tell him what its name was in English—'Gray-link!' said the *Fischer*—the proprietress of the Hotel Holy Ghost called my wife to help disentangle the excited *Fischer* and me from our language while she weighed the fish. It weighed exactly $1\frac{1}{4}$ kilos! Not a bad 'gray-link' for any part of the world.

Life was not all just one round of fun in that part of the world, not for me. I had gone down there that first summer, dead broke—£500 overdrawn at the bank, in fact—because I had just had a silly row with the new owner of a newspaper on which I had worked for eleven happy years. I had to make a new life. I had a book to write that, I knew (or at least I hoped), would be my shot in the locker. And that book had to be written. I never put on my trousers in the morning—except for two or three breaks of four days each when we were climbing between the ski-huts along the snows of the Italian frontier—until I had written ten pages. That was an unbroken vow. Meanwhile, my wife, my boy, and I lived on four shillings a day each. We had come down from England, 2nd and 3rd Class, without even sleepers. And it was after the day's work was done, usually around lunch time, that I would climb or fish.

But it was in the evening after dinner, when I should have been resting, that I found it the most fascinating time to fish. There was a bridge below the hotel, on the far side of which stood an ancient little whitewashed Catholic church. On its wall, too, facing the water, was a peasant painting of St. Christopher carrying Christ on his shoulder, wading knee deep through painted water as miraculously clear as the real water which flowed beneath his feet.

Here every evening was a rise of trout such as I would not have believed possible. You could stand on the bridge in the still spring nights and hear splash after splash after splash. . . . And if you waded out from the bushes at the foot of the ancient church, not caring if the water did come over your waders, you had fishing such as you might dream of in heaven. It was here that I used the unnamed fly tied by the Captain in the English Army of Occupation at Cologne. It was a whitish, hackled arrangement, with a grey body; and I fished it until there was little of it left except the bare hook. Its effectiveness increased with its bedraggled condition. Night after night I clumped back to the hotel, almost stupefied by my good luck—the miracle of that fly. And I would slide a bagful of beautiful fish out on the verandah table. In that dim porch light, with the reflection from the green vines, the beauty of those fish had something haunting about it. We loved to touch them, turn them over, pick them up, admire them. The silent shake of the old Austrian count's grey head had something reverent about it. Here was the Adoration of the Fish.

147

I state this solemnly. I have never had quite that hushed feeling about the trout anywhere else. And we all felt it. Then one night there was a terrific strike, my rod bent in the dark; it bent, it bent, it bent. . . . For you could not allow the fish to run into the rapids immediately below. And then it straightened out. The line came back empty. The fly was gone. I climbed up the bank by the church with the feeling that I was not meant to catch any more fish below the feet of St. Christopher painted on its walls.

I never did.